I0472331

Port Hope Ontario Book 1 in Colour Photos, Saving Our History One Photo at a Time

Photography
by Barbara Raué
©2019

Series Name: Cruising Ontario

Book 230: Port Hope Book 1

Cover photo: 160 Walton Street, Page 55

Series Name: Cruising Ontario
Saving Our History One Photo at a Time
in colour photos

Books Available in Alphabetical Order:
Aberfoyle, Acton, Ajax, Alton, Amherstburg, Ancaster, Arthur, Auburn, Aylmer, Ayr, Beaver Valley, Belgrave, Belleville, Bloomingdale, Blyth, Brantford, Brockville, Burford, Burlington, Caledon, Caledonia, Cambridge, Carlow, Chatsworth, Clifford, Collingwood, Conestogo, Delhi, Dorchester to Aylmer, Drayton, Drumbo, Dundas, Dunlop, Eden Mills, Elmira, Elora, Erin, Essex, Fergus, Goderich, Grimsby, Guelph, Hagersville, Hamilton, Hanover, Harriston, Hespeler, Jarvis, Kingston, Kingsville, Kitchener, Lake Superior, Lincoln, Linwood, Listowel, London, Lucknow, Merrickville, Mono, Mount Forest, Mount Pleasant, Neustadt, New Hamburg, Newboro, Newport, Niagara-on-the-Lake, Niagara Falls, North Bay, Oakville, Onondaga, Orangeville, Orillia, Oshawa, Owen Sound, Palmerston, Paris, Pelham, Perth, Peterborough, Petrolia, Pickering, Port Colborne, Port Elgin, Portland, Preston, Rockwood, Sarnia, Sault Ste. Marie, Seaforth, Sheffield, Shelburne, Simcoe, Smiths Falls, Smithville, Southampton, St. Catharines, St. George, St. Jacobs, St. Marys, St. Thomas, Stoney Creek, Stratford, Thamesford, Thunder Bay, Tillsonburg, Toronto, Waterdown, Waterford, Waterloo, Welland, Wellesley, West Flamborough, Westport, Whitby, Windsor, Wingham, Woodstock

Table of Contents

Port Hope is a heritage community situated on the north shore of Lake Ontario in Northumberland County and offers both an urban and rural paradise with the perfect combination of heritage charm, modern vibrancy and cultural allure. The Ganaraska River runs through the heart of town past historic buildings.

The Township was opened in 1792 and named in honor of Colonel Henry Hope, a member of the Legislative Council of Canada.

Before Canada became a nation in 1867, Port Hope was already a boomtown. Its main streets were thronged with horse-drawn carriages and farmers' wagons, its plank sidewalks crowded with shoppers and merchandise. Wood-burning locomotives pulled heavily loaded trains through town on their way to a harbor filled with schooners and steamships. Solid brick commercial blocks and houses lined the streets.

The town grew rapidly from four families of English descent who arrived by boat in 1793 and settled at the river mouth. Until then the area had been home to aboriginal groups — Huron, then Iroquois, and finally Mississauga — attracted by the salmon and sturgeon that swarmed in its river.

The first European settlers came from the new United States. They had chosen to follow the British crown after the American Revolution. So had Elias Smith, a Montreal merchant who, with two partners, Jonathan and Abraham Walton, financed their arrival. In return for settling forty families on the land and building a sawmill and flourmill to serve them, the partners received a grant of land roughly the size of modern urban Port Hope.

More families arrived including blacksmiths, carpenters, bricklayers, and merchants. The mills drew farmers from fifty and sixty kilometers away. Grain that could not be milled was bought by distilleries — there were eventually five along the river — that produced a famous Port Hope whisky. Its most rapid growth began when railways revolutionized travel in what is now Ontario. In 1856 the Grand Trunk Railway connected Port Hope to Toronto and the Atlantic seaboard. Its viaduct over the Ganaraska River was the second greatest engineering challenge on the route, exceeded only by bridging the St. Lawrence River at Montreal.

Another railway heading north from Port Hope opened up the vast timberlands and new farms of central Ontario and stretched to Peterborough and Lindsay. Eventually it reached Georgian Bay, at Midland. Down this line came great loads of timber and grain. Some went east to England, but most was exported to the USA through Rochester across the lake.

Walton Street was named after Captain Jonathan Walton who brought the first settlers here. The Walton and Smith families were among the original petitioners for land grants and figured very prominently in the Town's history. Port Hope was incorporated as a police village in 1834.

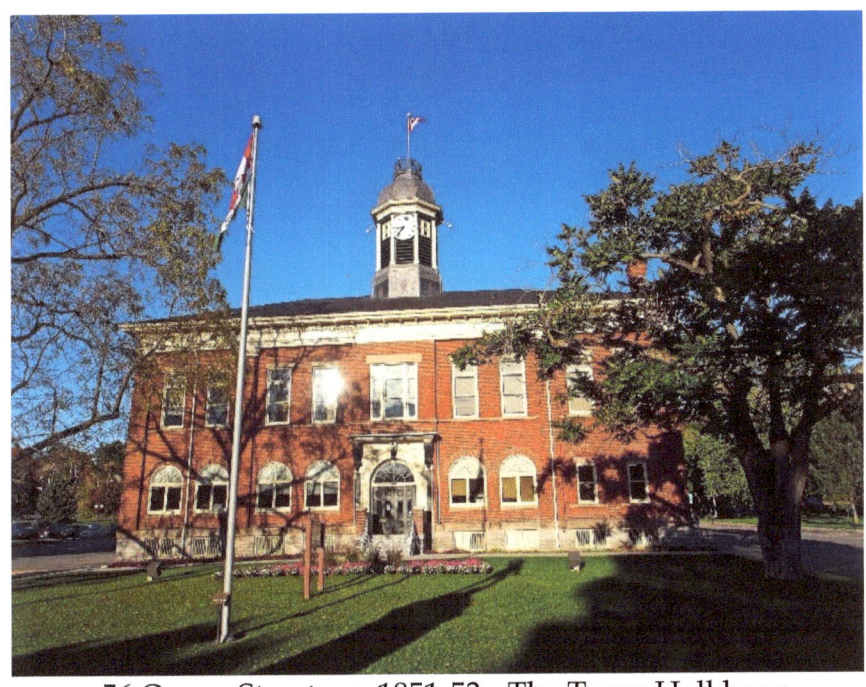

56 Queen Street – c. 1851-53 - The Town Hall has a center entrance with a round-headed fan-lighted transom on its seven-bay pilastered front. The building was designed in the Neo-Classical style. The central octagonal cupola has alternating four-paned, heavily mullioned transomed windows, and clock faces with Roman numerals. Louvred panels are separated by small slender Roman Doric colonettes.

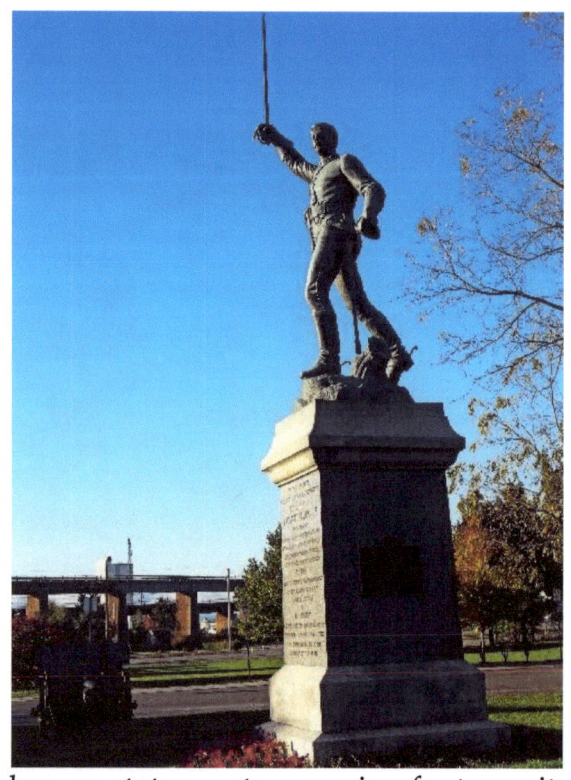

The bronze statue rests on a nine-foot granite pedestal. The inscription reads: "To Commemorate the Devoted Patriotism and Heroic Bravery of Lieutenant Colonel Arthur T. H. Williams, M.P. Commanding the Midland Battalion of Volunteer Militia who after gallantly leading the victorious and decisive charge at the Battle of Batoche, during the rebellion in the North West Territories dies of sickness contracted in the discharge of his duty near Fort Pitt, N.W.T. on the 4th July 1885. This monument is erected in his native Town by his admiring countrymen throughout Canada assisted by his companions in arms, and the Government of the Dominion of Canada."

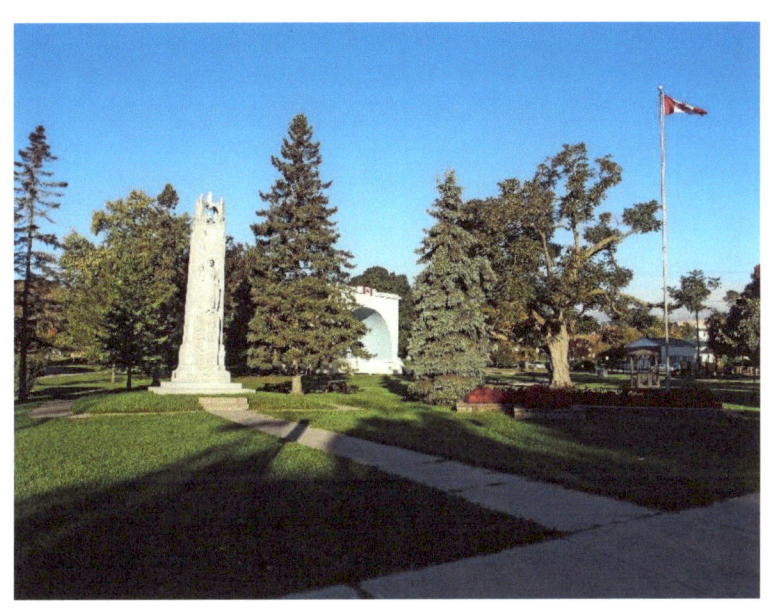

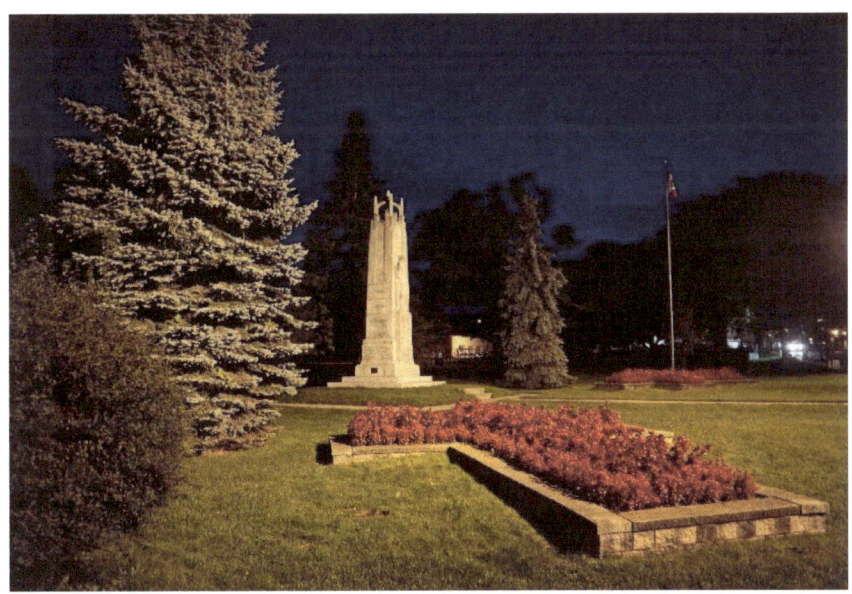

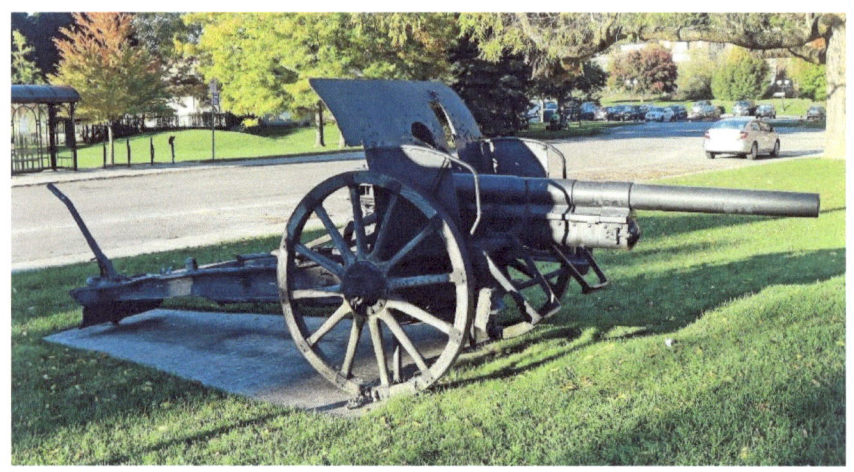

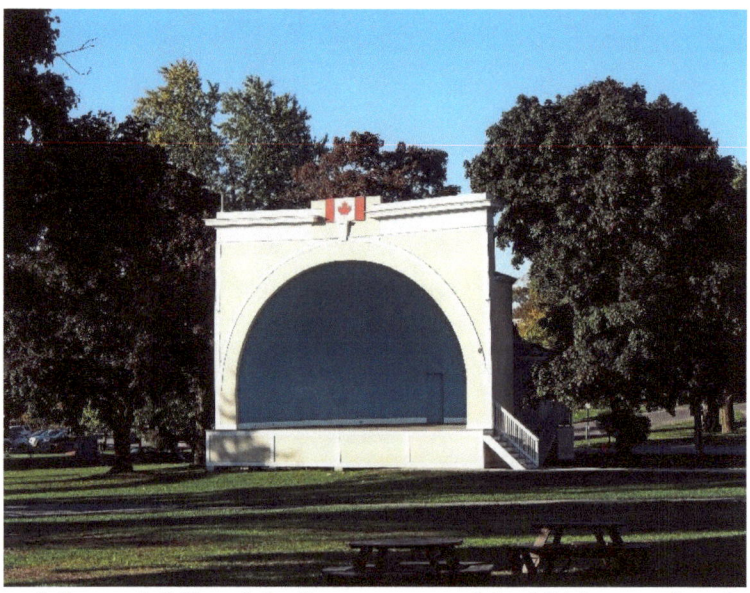

Memorial Bandshell constructed in 1946 – made of stucco – to honour the members of all armed forces who fought in all wars since Canada's confederation in 1867

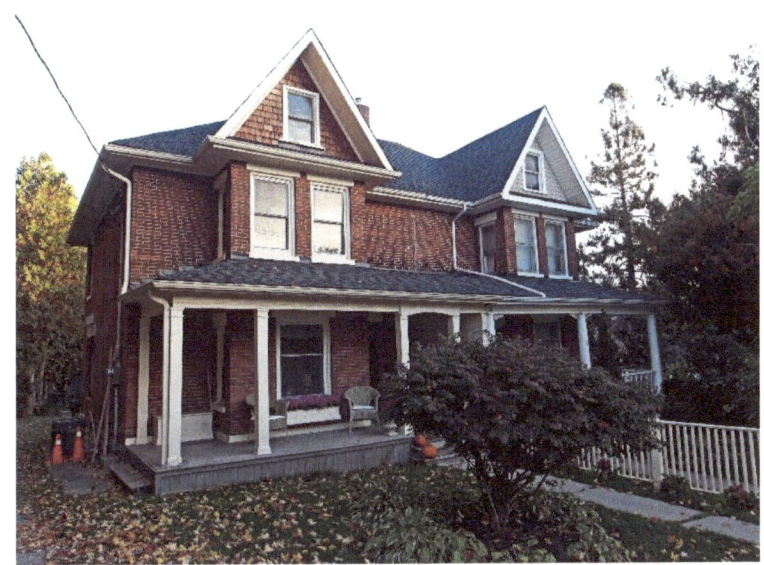

6 Bedford Street

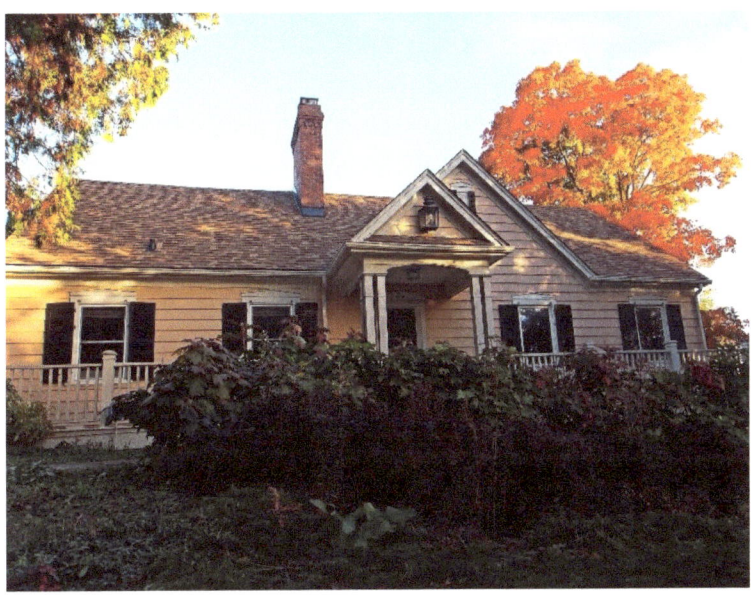

16 Bedford Street - pediment

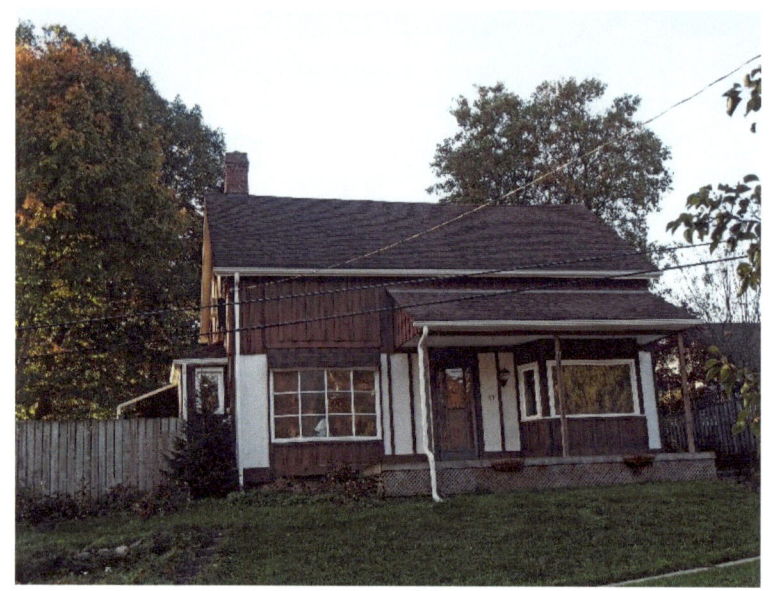

17 Bedford Street

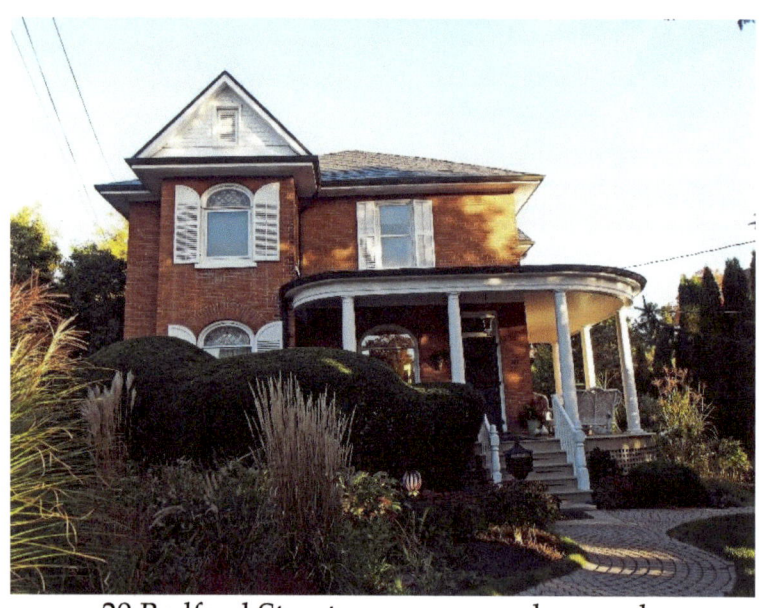

20 Bedford Street – wraparound veranda

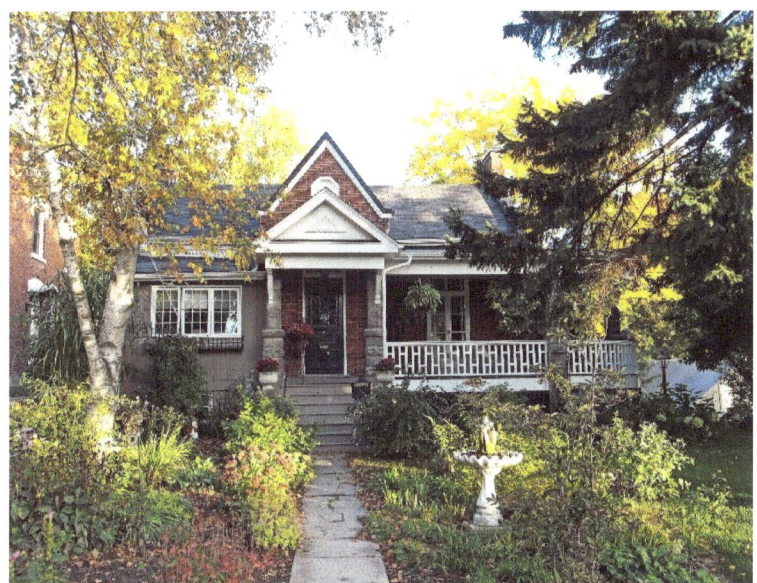

24 Bedford Street – Coolmount Cottage – wraparound veranda, pediment with decorated tympanum, octagonal blind window in gable, transom window above door

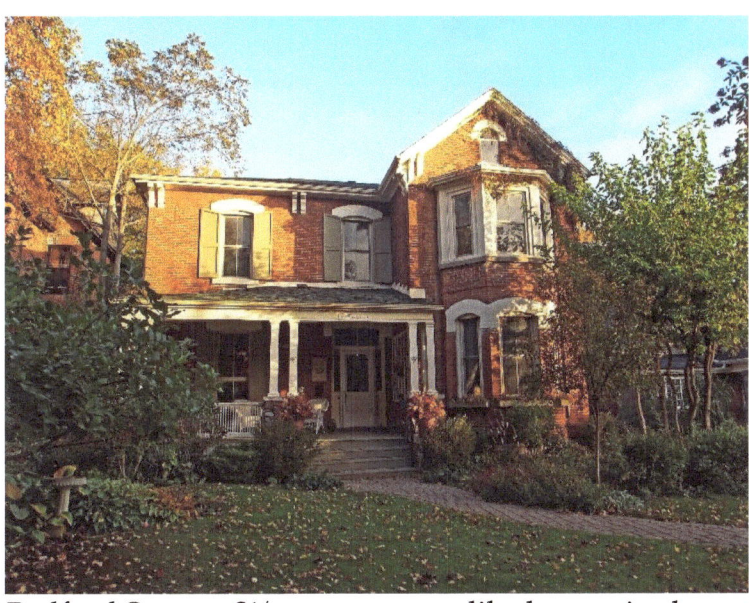

26 Bedford Street – 2½-storey tower-like bay, paired cornice brackets, sidelights, transom

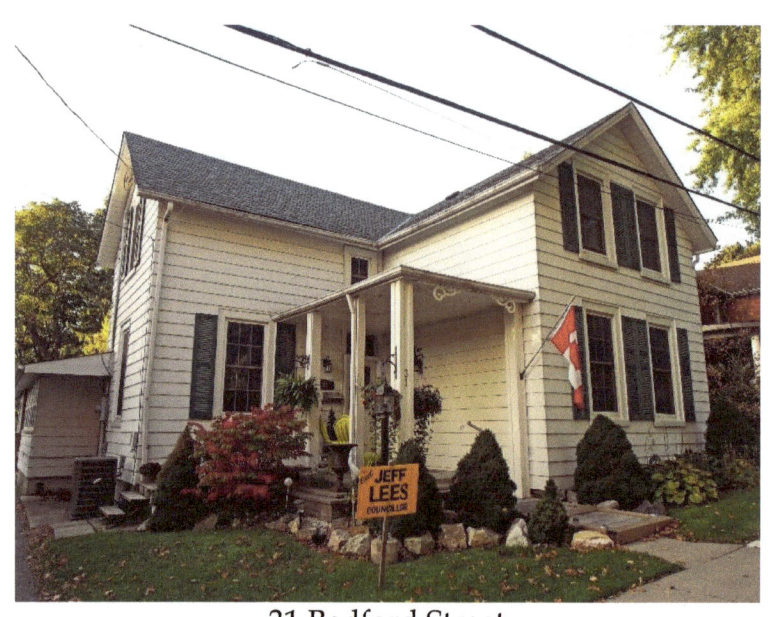

31 Bedford Street

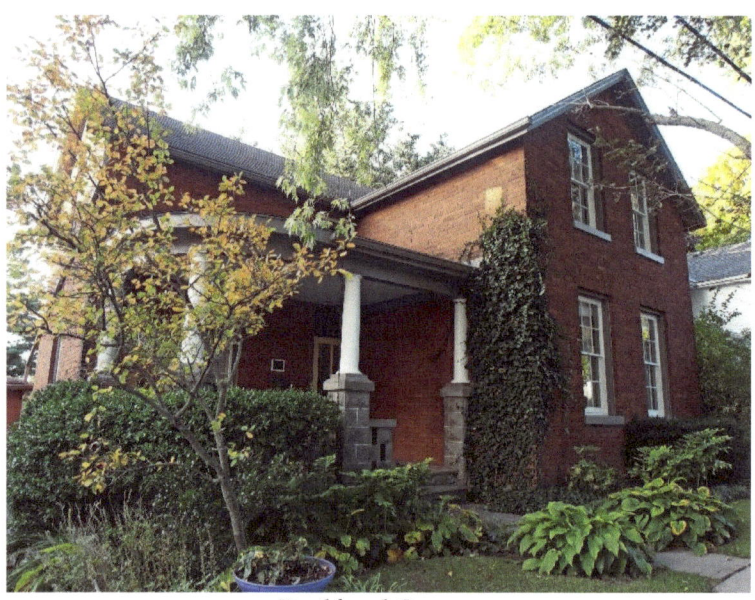

Bedford Street

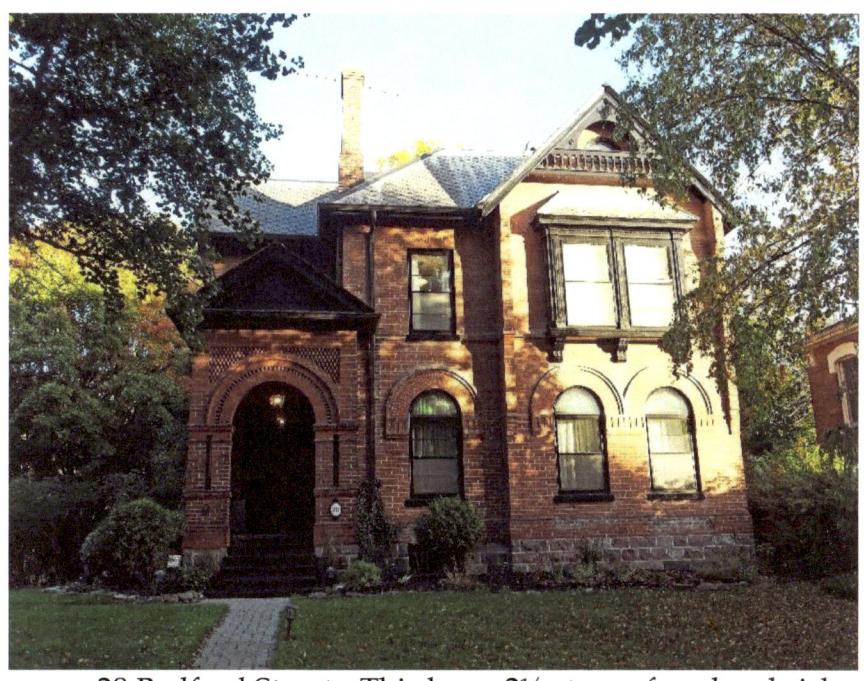

28 Bedford Street - This large 2½ storey four bay brick house is built in the Romanesque Revival style with a large irregular plan, heavy masonry, steeply pitched roof, tall chimneys, recessed porch, and oriel windows. The imposing entranceway is composed of a shingled pediment and round arches of corbelled and stepped brick with decorative panels on either side of corbelled brick.

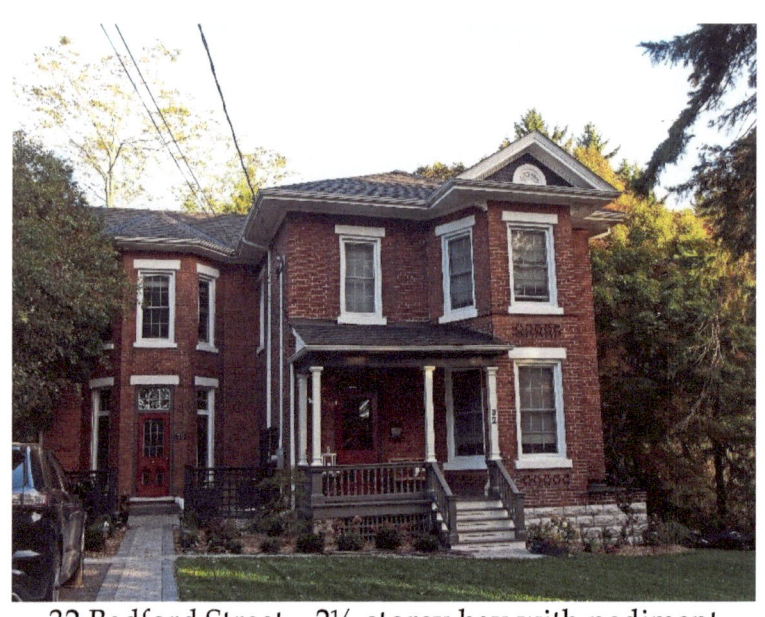

32 Bedford Street – 2½-storey bay with pediment

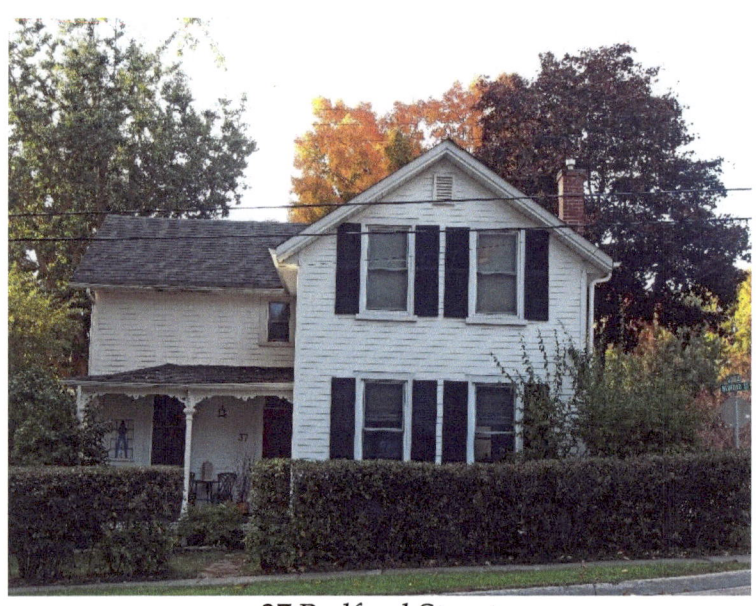

37 Bedford Street

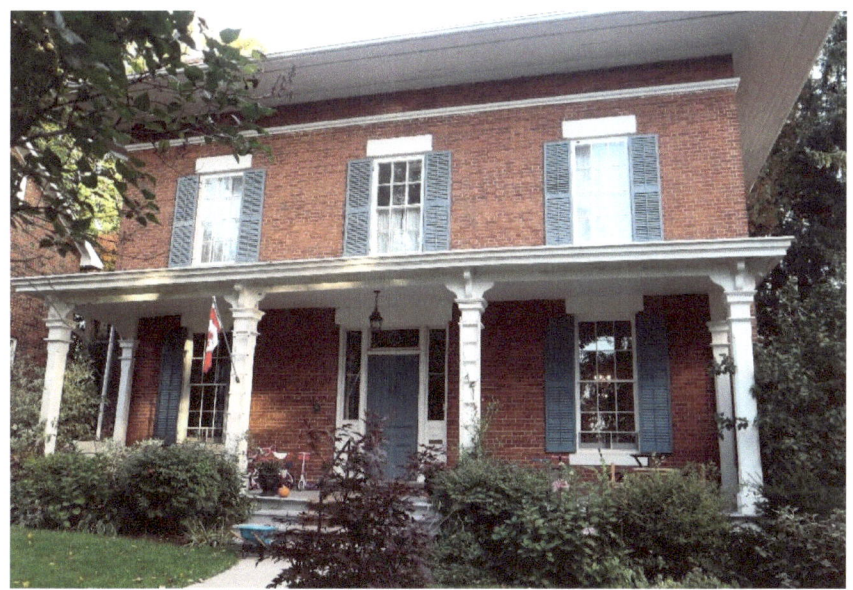

42 Bedford Street – c. 1860 – mid-Victorian style - two storeys high with a hipped roof with extended eaves; wood band decoration below the cornice; transom and sidelights around front door; collared polygonal posts on the full-width veranda

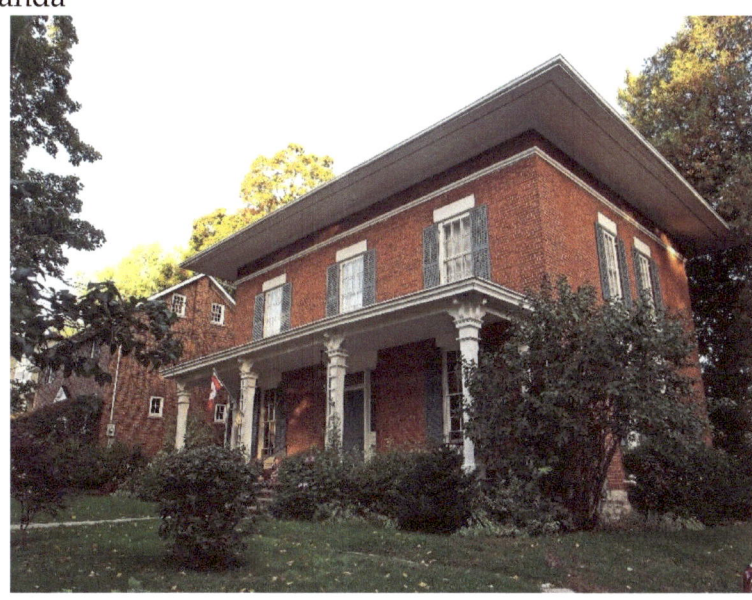

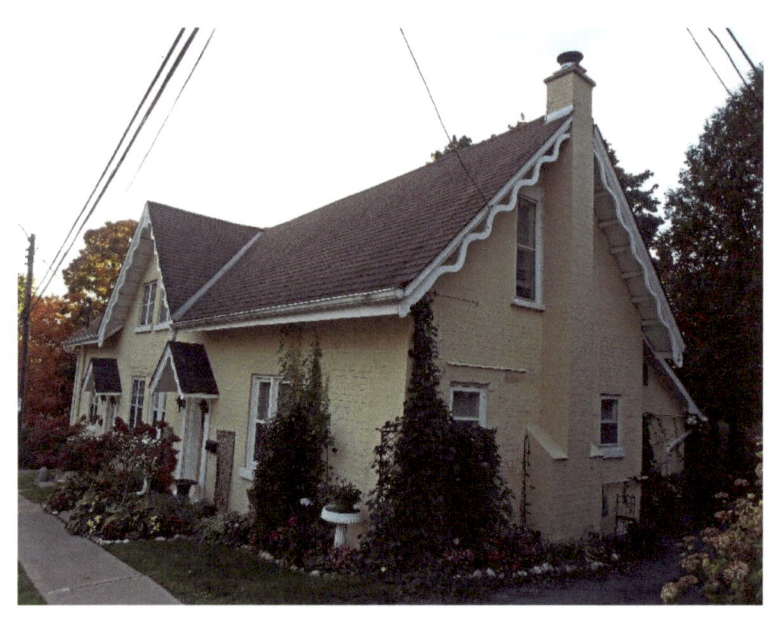

43-45 Bedford Street – Gothic - verge board trim on gables

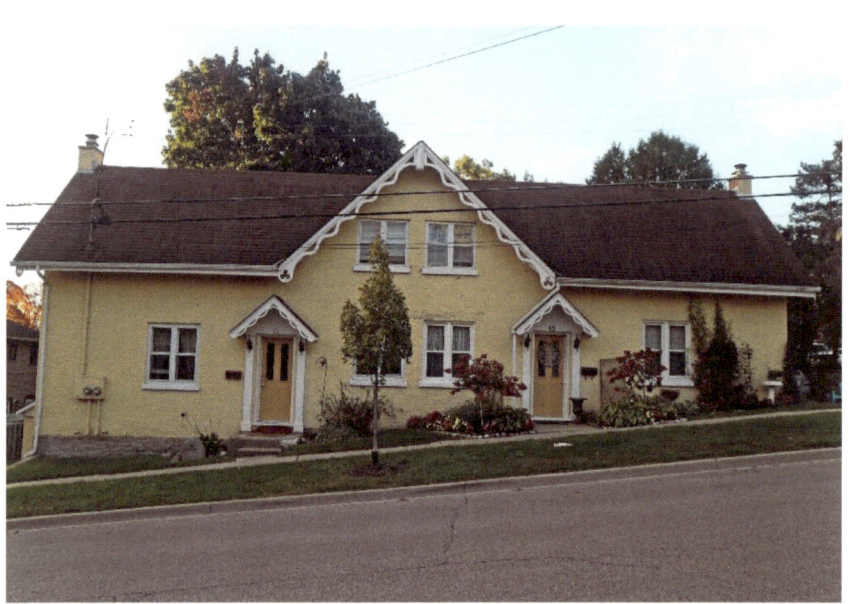

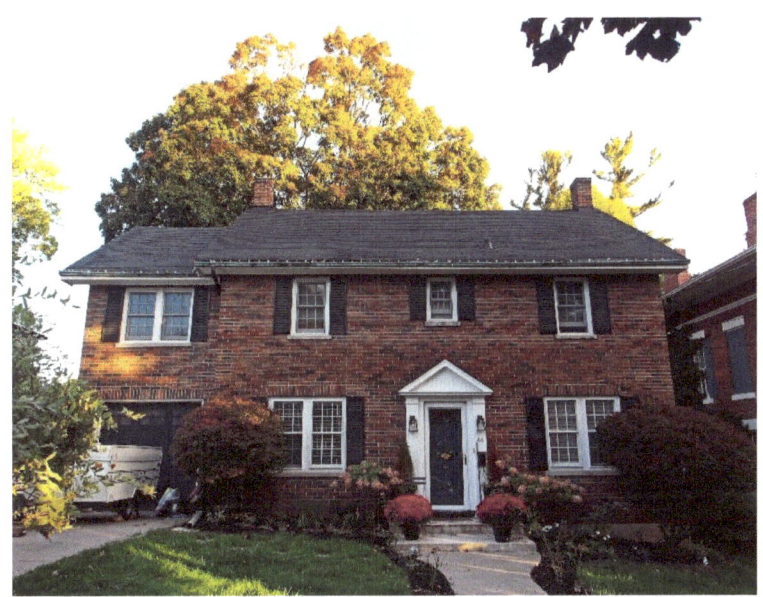

44 Bedford Street – Georgian style – multipaned windows, pediment above entrance

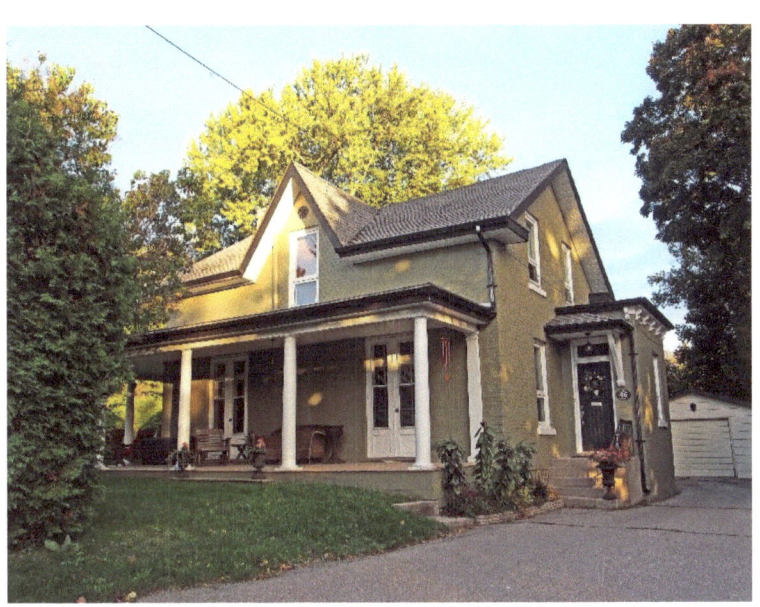

46 Bedford Street - Gothic

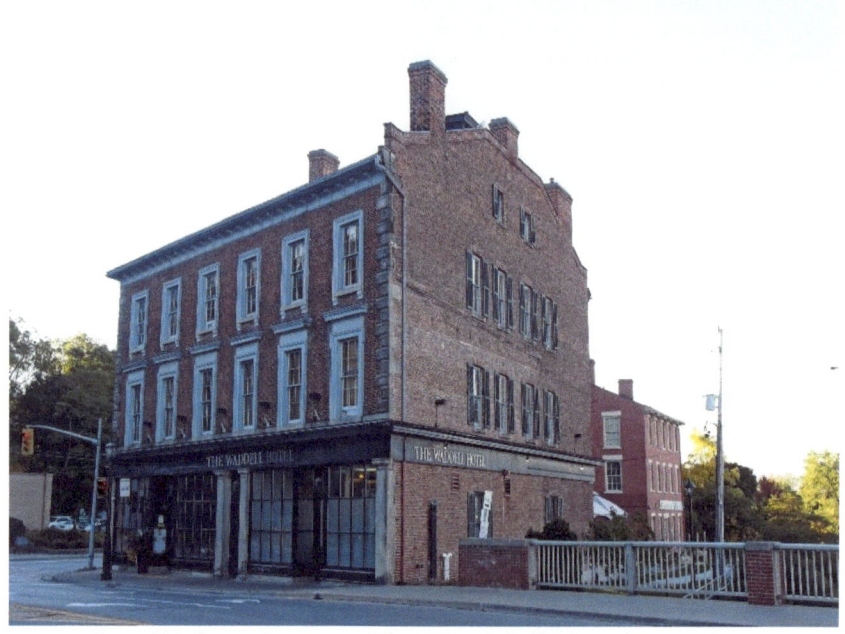

One Walton Street – The Waddell Hotel – c. 1845 - This three-storey brick ell-shaped commercial block with residential space above fronts to Walton and Mill Streets. Its handsome facades include stone columns, pilasters and lintels at the ground floor level, rusticated stone quoins, eared wood window surrounds with cornices to architraves at the second floor, and a simpler treatment with wood surrounds to openings on the third storey. The roof is gabled and turning the corner forms a hip.

The Ganaraska River originally divided into two streams around the present Walton Street Bridge and the area where this building stands was an island. When the river was re-channeled the entire Mill Street area was built up from marsh and became another access route to the harbour. In 1844, Robert Needham Waddell had this prominent corner block constructed.

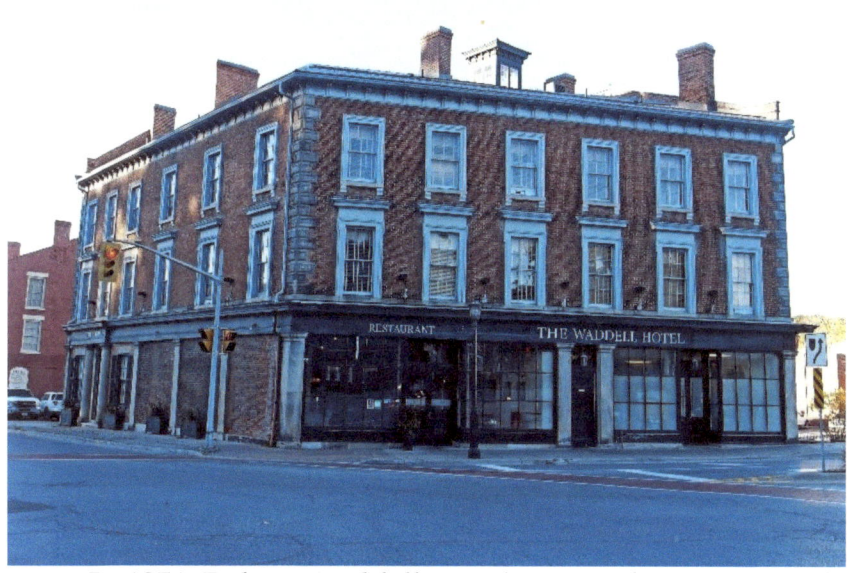

    In 1851, Robert Waddell was the agent for the Bank of Montreal, which was located in the Waddell Block, and he had a dry goods, grocery and hardware store. In the early 1850's, he had a flouring and gristmill on Mill Street capable of producing two hundred barrels a day with six runs of stone. His operation included two frame buildings, one four storey and one five storey building. He became a director of the Port Hope, Lindsay and Peterborough Railway in 1853. He was the local sheriff for many years and later became the sheriff of Northumberland and Durham residing in Cobourg.

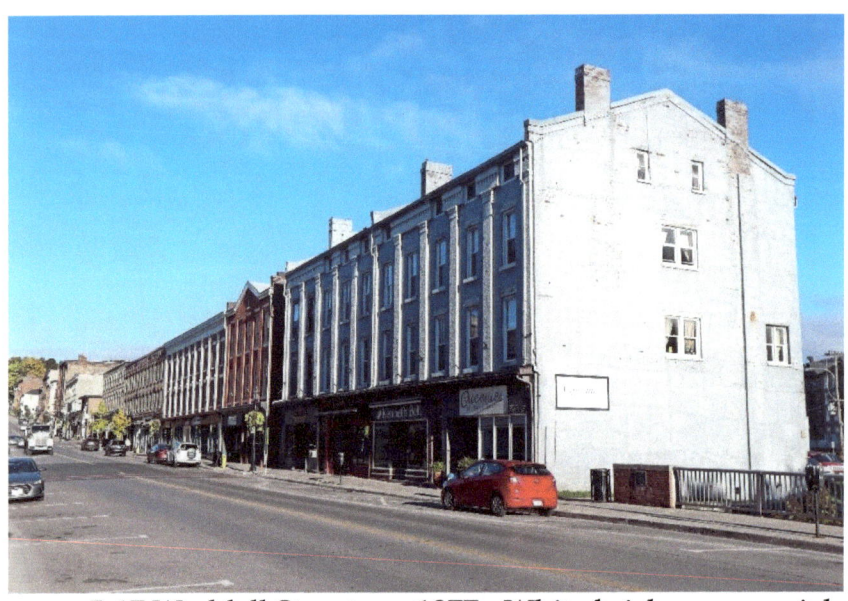

5-17 Waddell Street – c. 1877 - White brick commercial block with stores below and storage space above in six units. This building was in the mid-Victorian style, but still carried the local details of ornamental brickwork, including labels over segmental window heads, a band course serving as a shop front cornice and heavily modelled parapet fronting the low-pitched shed roof.

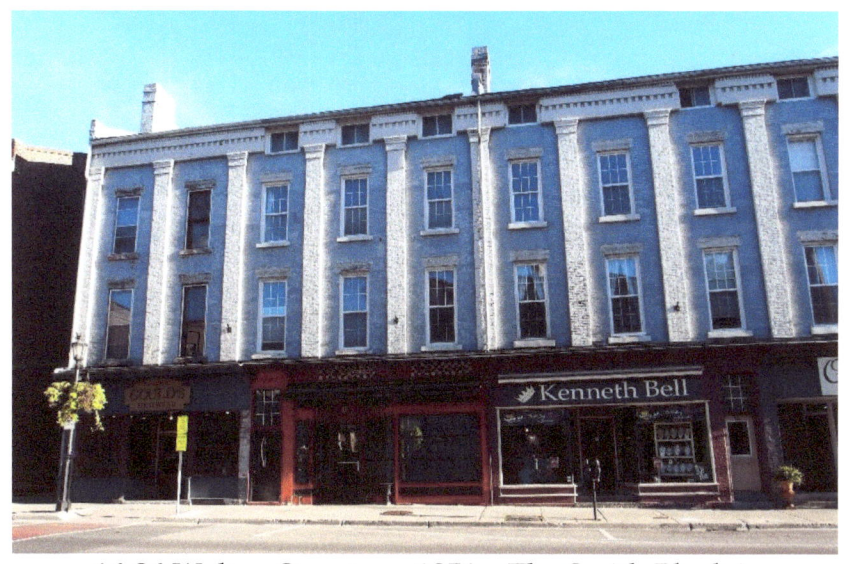

16-26 Walton Street – c. 1851 – The Smith Block is situated on land that was part of the estate of John David Smith, land which he had earlier received from his father, Elias Smith, one of the holders of the original Crown Land Grants.

This brick commercial building with residential and/or storage space above, three storeys high is the typical pilastered design of the mid-19th century with ornamental brickwork to cornice and frieze.

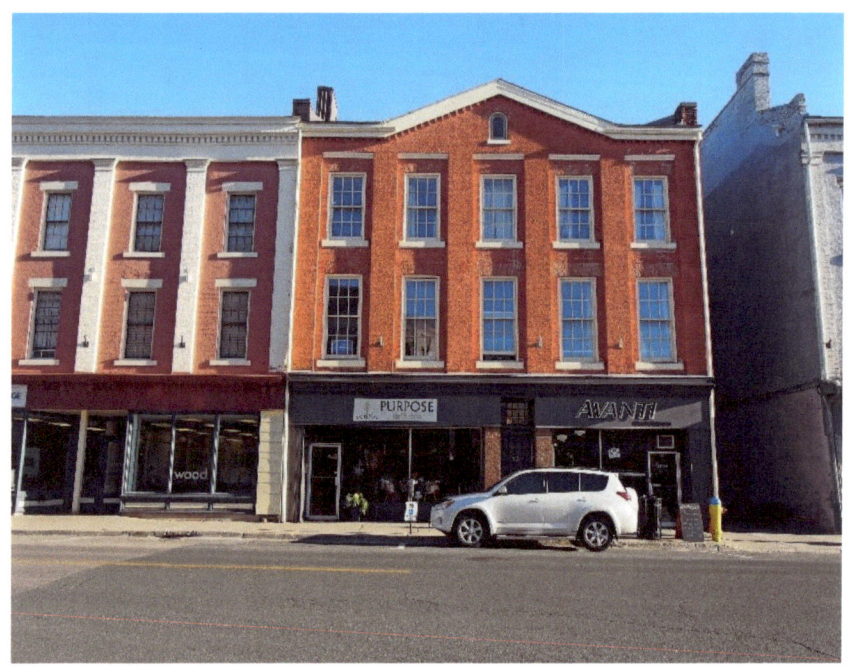

28-32 Walton Street – c. 1844 - This block is a brick three-storey hotel building built in a favoured position as a focal point to the end of Queen Street. This building retains the central gable with recessed panels to the front creating a simple pilastered design of five bays, complete with brick cornice and end chimneys, original sash in the upper storeys. The centre gable has a semi-circular gable window with radiating voussoirs and a wooden lugsill.

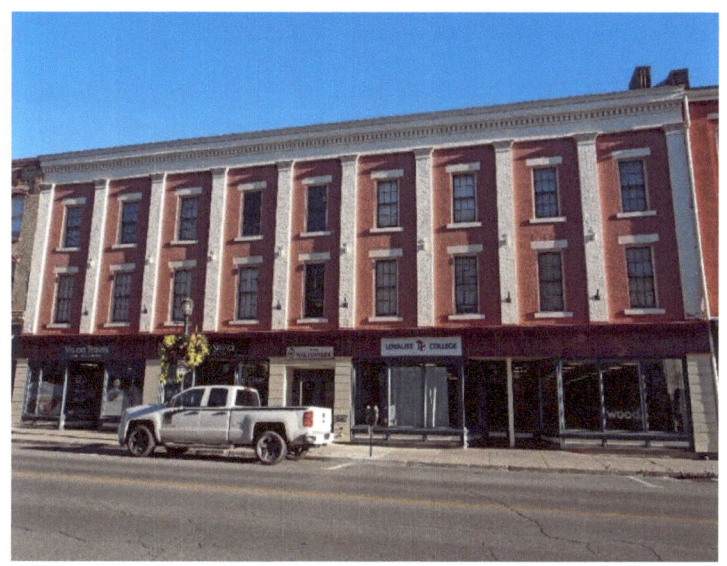

34-36 Walton Street – c. 1850 - The Smith Block is a brick commercial block with three storeys in five units with brick pilasters capped with wood. The early decorative treatment of contrasting pilasters and cornice in cream and recessed panels in red may reflect the original brickwork.

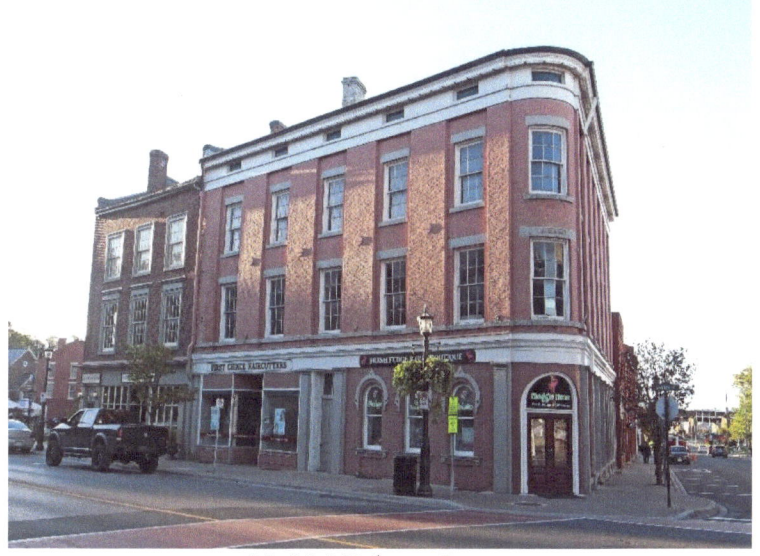

29-33 Walton Street

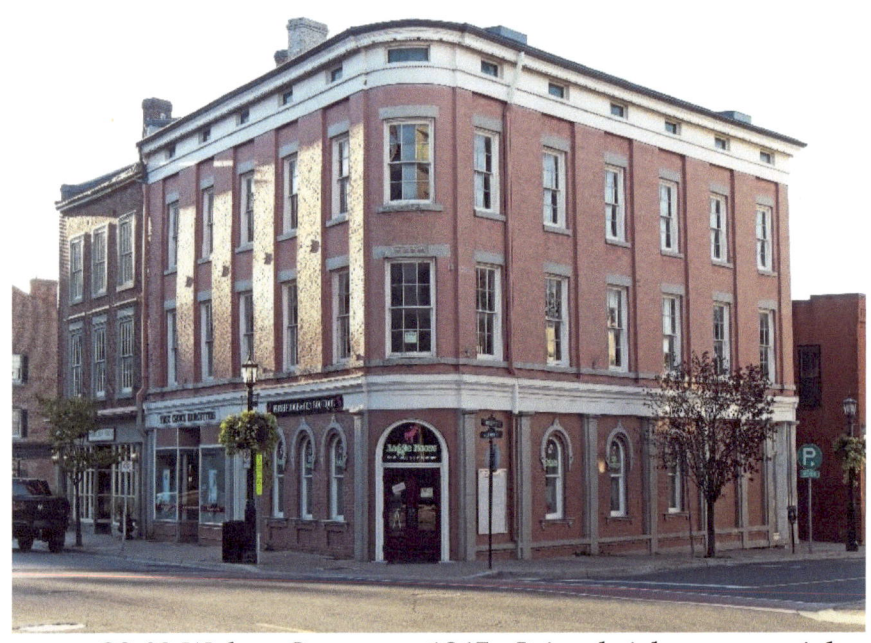

29-33 Walton Street – c. 1845 - It is a brick commercial building with residential and/or storage space above. The corner is rounded to Queen and Walton Streets, and the block stands three storeys high. A pilastered front of Greek Revival style is topped by a heavy wooden frieze and cornice. The frieze is pierced by stomachers, and the soffit contains mutules and guttae, characteristic of Greek Revival. There are six bays to the Walton Street facade, including one on the rounded corner, and six bays to the Queen Street facade. The windows on the second and third storeys are headed by a plain lintel and supported by lugsills on the third storey and a continuous sill, acting as a string course on the second storey.

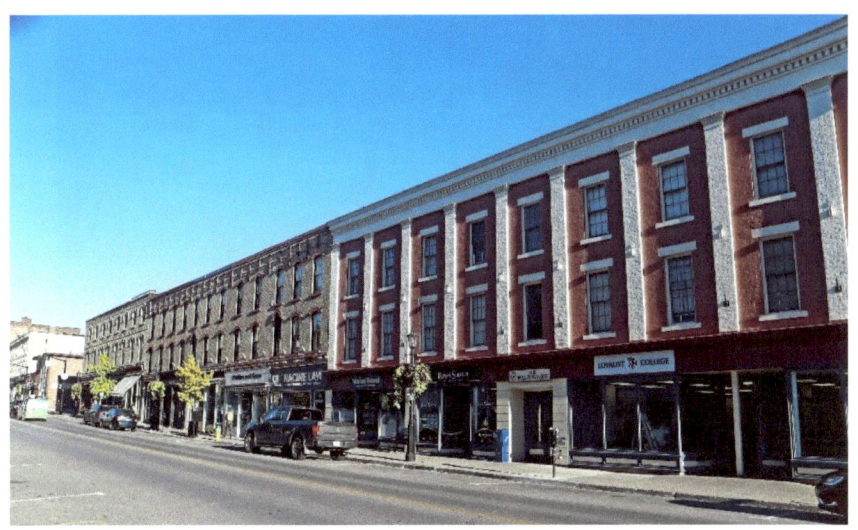

36-60 Walton Street

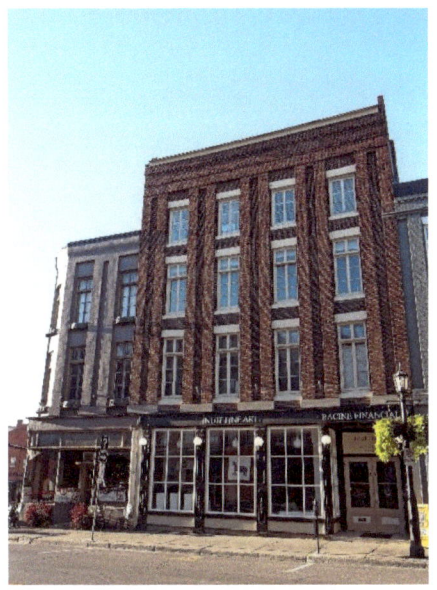

37 Walton Street – c. 1850 – This is a four-storey brick commercial building with commercial and/or storage space above with a low-pitched shed roof. The stone-based twinned pilasters and narrow recesses to windows are crowned by an ornamental brick cornice with projecting dentils.

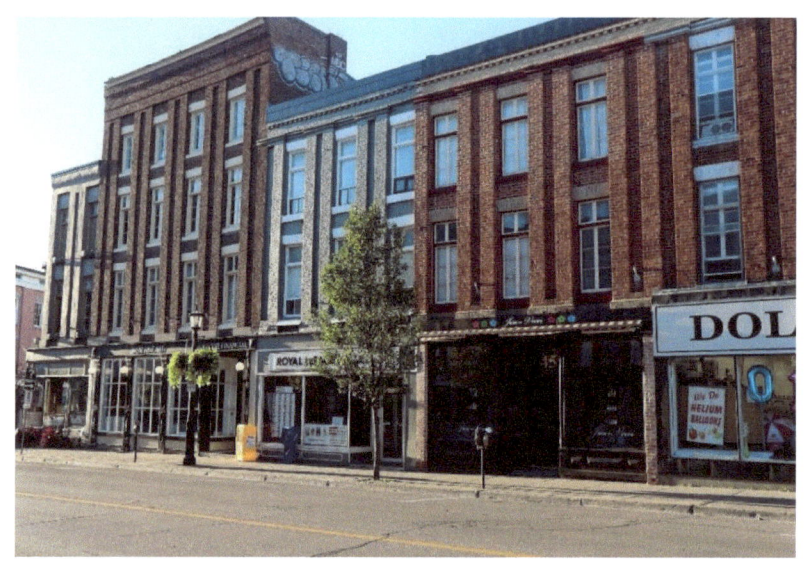
37-45 Walton Street

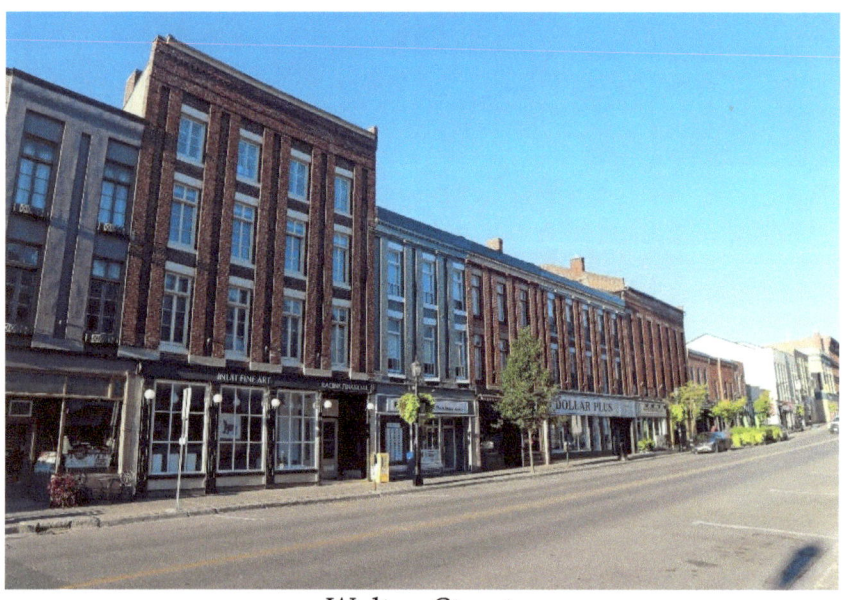
Walton Street

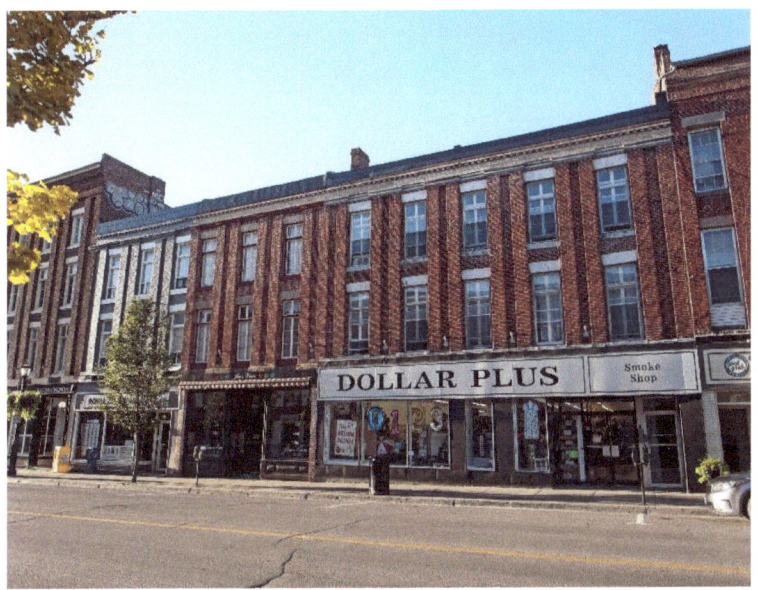

41-51 Walton Street – c. 1850 - This is a three-storey brick commercial block with residential and/or storage space above. The low-gabled parapet roof meets a brick cornice with projecting dentils.

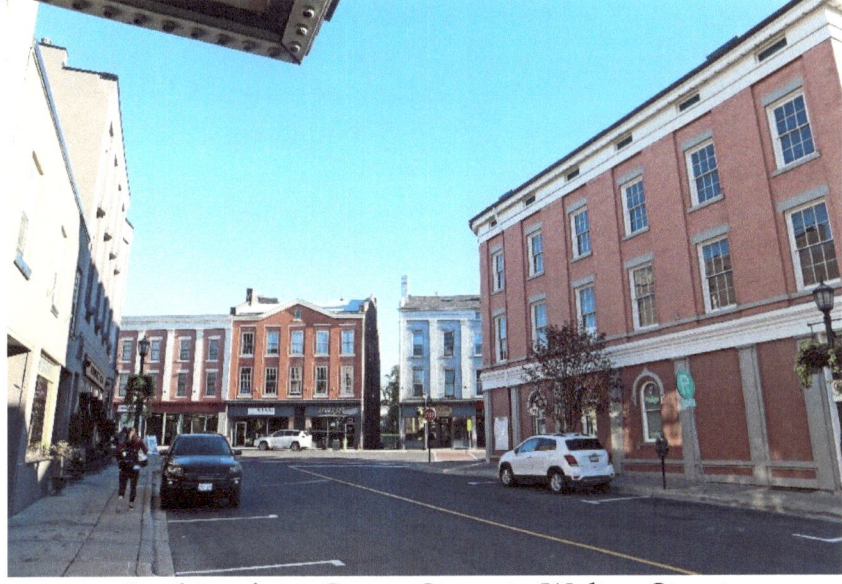

Looking from Queen Street to Walton Street

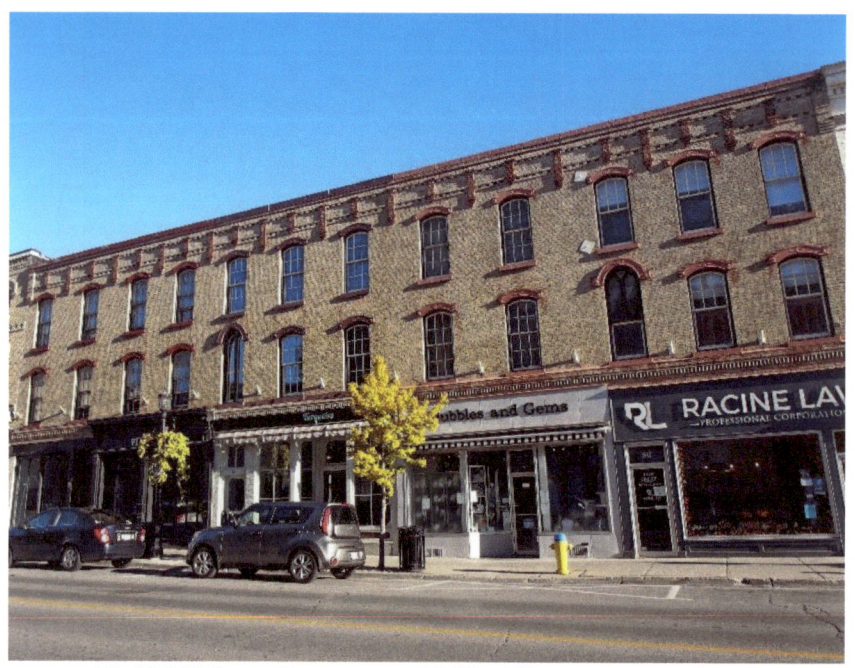

48-60 Walton Street – c. 1867 – There are twelve bays in each of the two upper storeys, most of which have semi-elliptical structural openings, with corresponding cast iron segmental labels. The two exceptions are found on the second storey and are relatively elongated semi-circular decorative windows. The stairwells, which provided access to the upper floors, were located behind the two long windows, thereby sectioning the block into two sections each with two short bays, the long bay in the centre, and then two short bays. Along the roof line is an ornamental brick cornice known as a machicolated or bracketed cornice, featuring two heavy anchoring brackets at either end of the block; two courses of dentilling; and alternate short/long bracketing throughout.

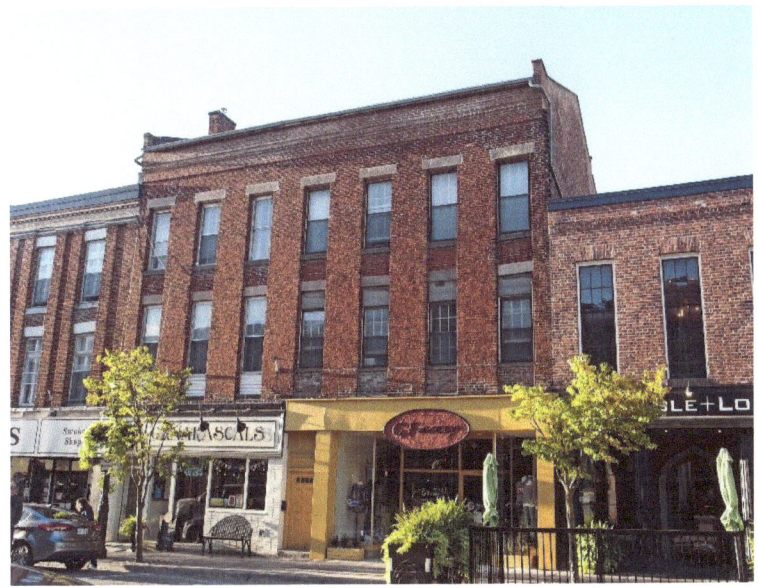

53-57 Walton Street – c. 1850 - This is a three-storey brick commercial block with residential and/or storage space above. Piers separating the window recesses in the upper storeys run to the top of the third storey where the wall becomes a continuous band with elaborate brickwork to the cornice.

Henry Howard Meredith acquired the land upon which several blocks were built on Walton Street. He was a prominent figure in Port Hope. He was a native of Ireland who came to Canada in 1829. In 1840, he married Margaret Brown, the third daughter of John Brown, a notable early settler. John Brown came to Port Hope from Cavan Ireland via the United States in 1818.

Meredith, along with his father-in-law, John Brown, and brother-in-law, James Madison Andrews, ran the Port Hope Harbour and Wharf Company until 1851 when the Board of Harbour Commissioners was established. Meredith was secretary for the Company from 1829 to 1851.

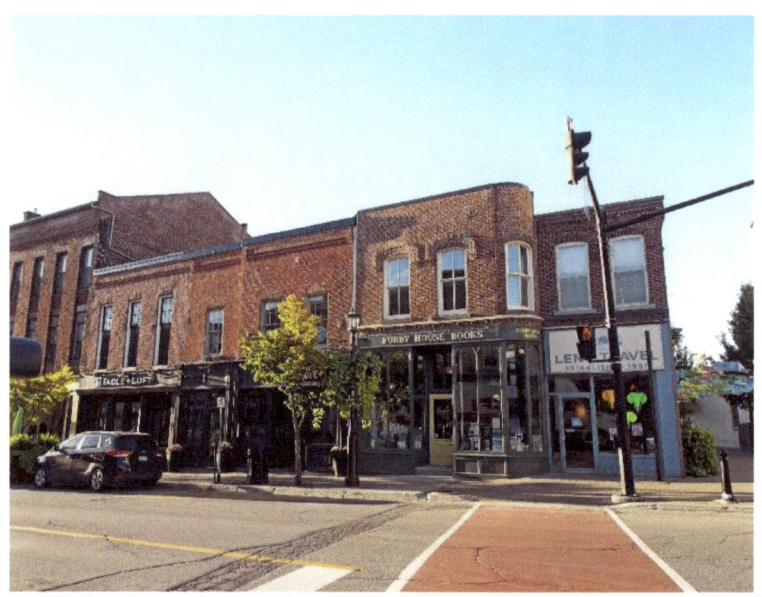

59 Walton Street (c. 1855) is a brick commercial block with assembly or storage space above. It is two storeys high in a single unit and appears as a truncated form of 53-57 Walton Street, never having been constructed to the third-floor level. A patterned brick parapet shields the shed roof while the cornice is a simple design. Three bays wide, its long, narrow windows are now blocked over.

63 Walton Street (c. 1865) is a two-storey brick commercial block.

65 Walton Street (c. 1871) is a two-storey brick commercial block, but was originally three storeys. It was the original corner block to the railway tracks before 67 Walton Street was built. The second storey has three bays to the main facade, including one on the rounded corner. The windows are segmentally headed with projecting brick labels and are supported by lugsills.

67 Walton Street (c. 1885) is set in behind the rounded corner of 65 Walton. Alexander W. Pringle was a watchmaker and a jeweller.

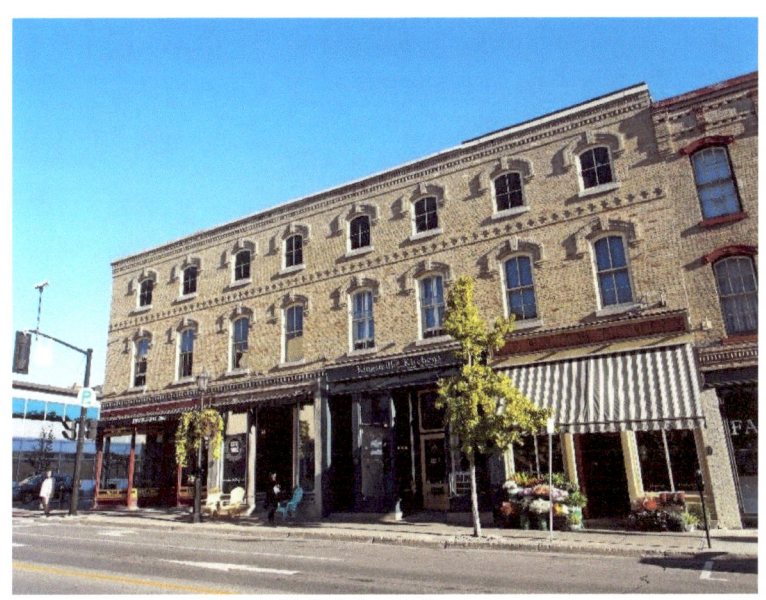

64 Walton Street

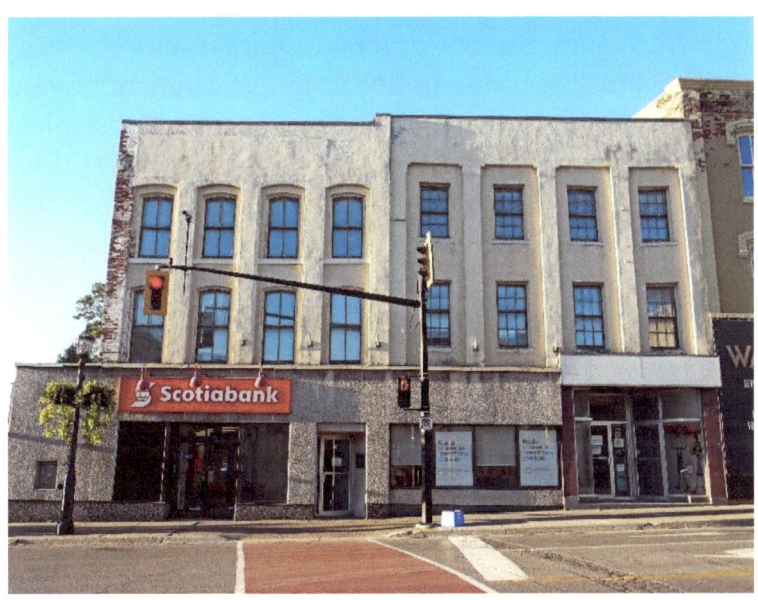

71 Walton Street

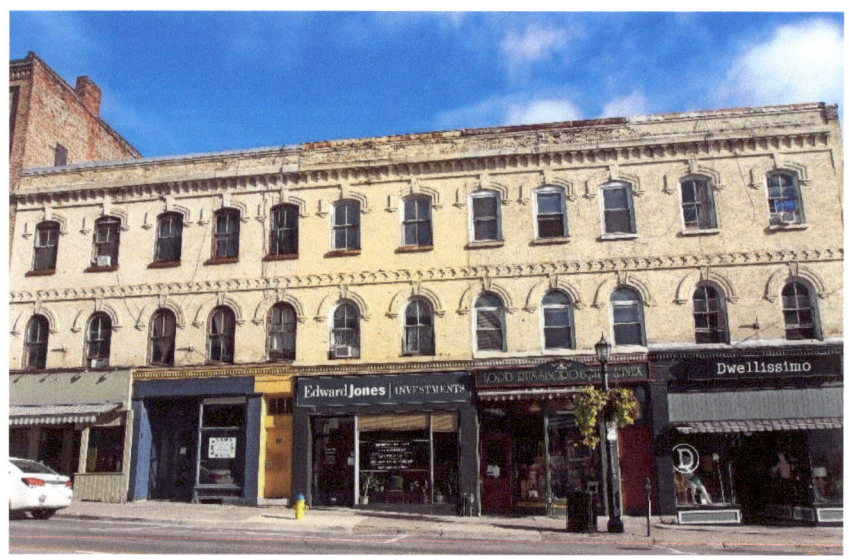

78-92 Walton Street – c. 1866 – Quinlan Block - This is a three-storey brick building in five sections. There are twelve semi-circular bays on the second storey and twelve semi-elliptical bays on the third storey. The facade of the building has several ornamental features, namely, a shop front cornice of dogtoothing, a horizontal course of ornamental brick work between the second and third storey, formed by rows of stretcher, header, stretcher, to create a series of crosses or diapers, a bracketed cornice constructed in a panelled brick parapet. The date marker is found in the keystone of the third storey bay, numbered sixth from the east.

Cornelius Quinlan (1822-1883) was a successful tinsmith and merchant.

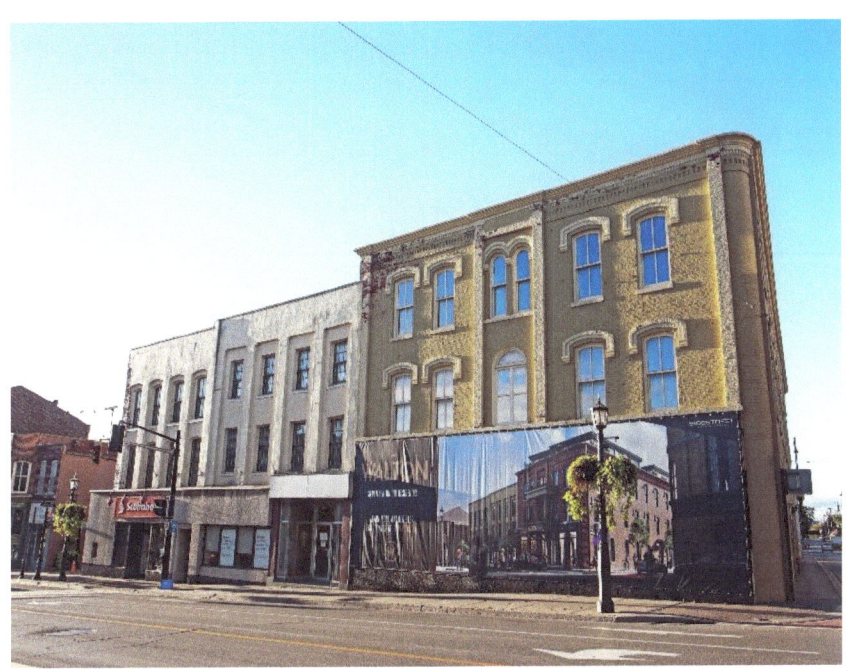

81 Walton Street - The Walton Hotel, formerly known as the Queen's Hotel, was built in 1870. A storey was added in 1876 and in 1907, a storey was also added on the south end of the building. As it stands today, the Walton Hotel is a three-storey brick building on the southeast corner of the intersection of John and Walton Streets. The Walton Street facade is divided in three sections by brick pilasters that carry through the ornamental brick cornice. The narrower central panel contains parted round-headed windows on the third floor surmounted by an ornamental name panel. Below is a round-headed window. Both side panels are identical on the second and third floors and contain paired windows with segmental heads and two-tier brick labels. The upper windows have individual sills whereas the second-floor ones share a continuous sill. An intricate brick cornice extends along the Walton Street facade as well as along John Street. The Walton Street corner of the building is rounded.

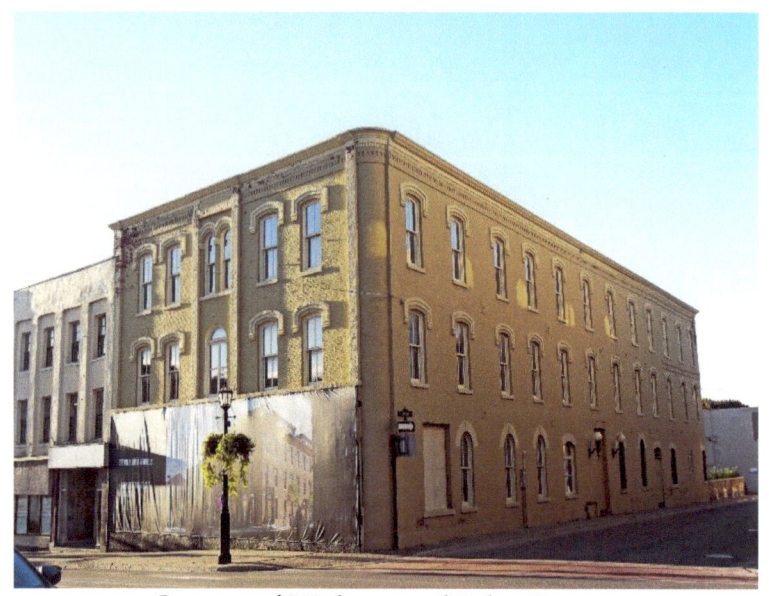

Corner of Walton and John Streets

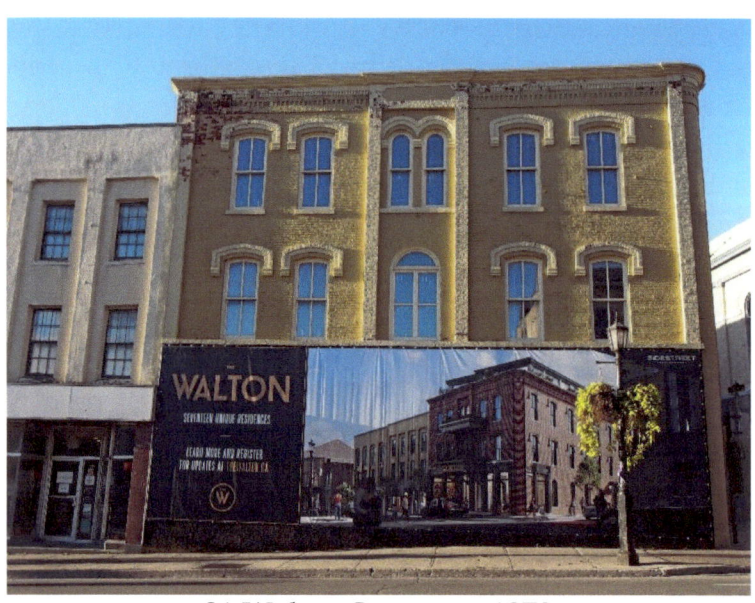

81 Walton Street – c. 1870

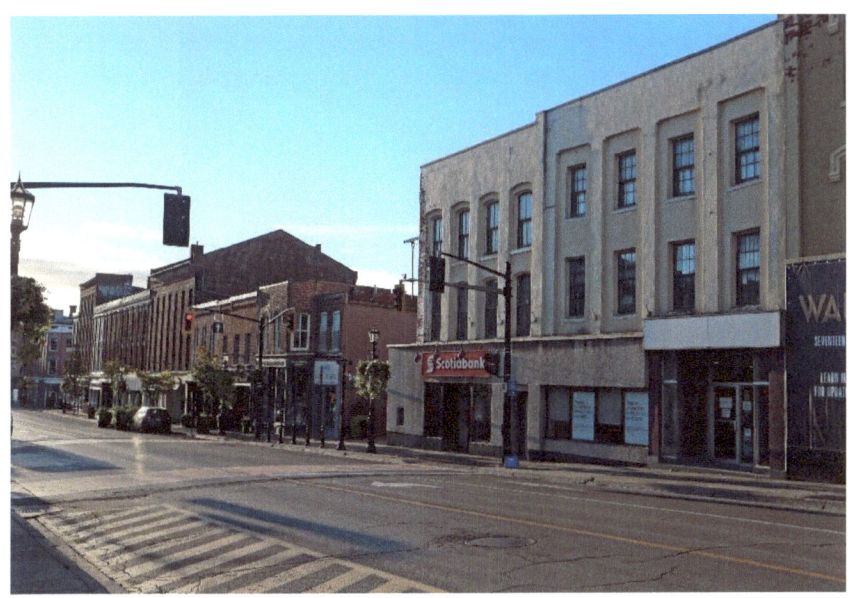

Walton Street

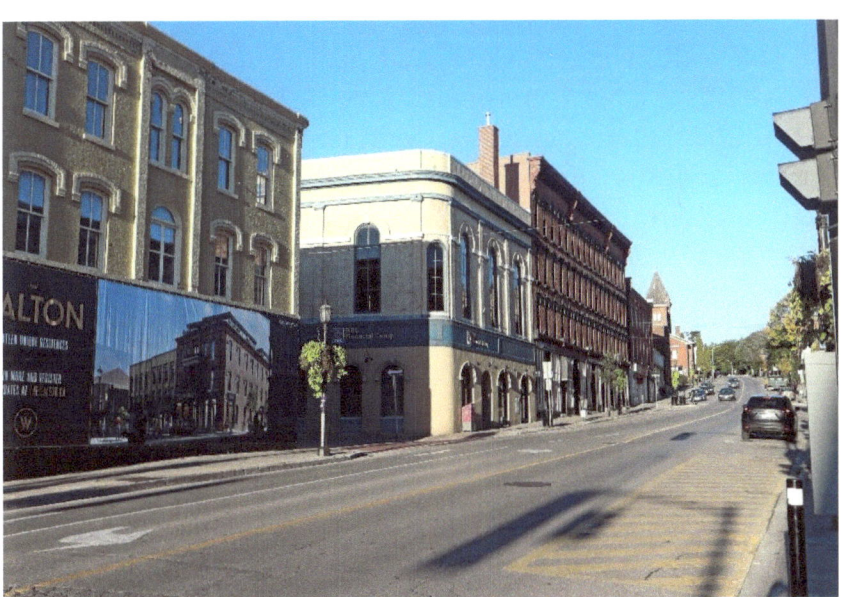

Walton Street

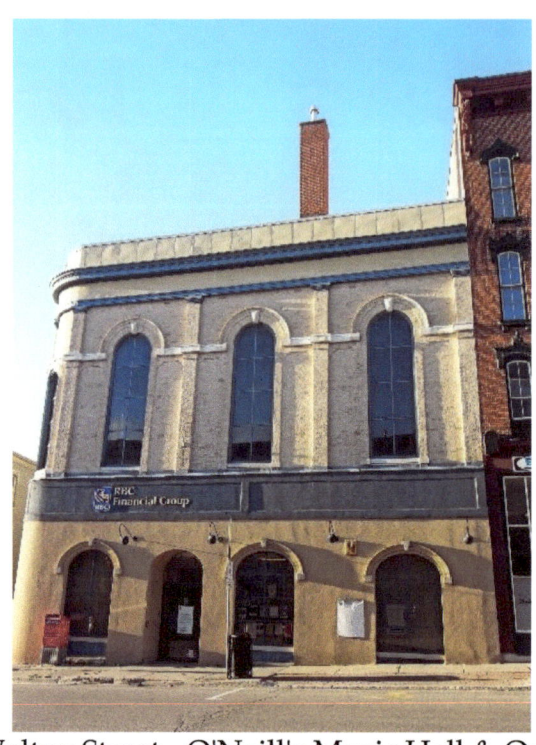

85 Walton Street - O'Neill's Music Hall & Opera Block –
c. 1871 - This is a brick commercial block, two storeys high in a
single unit. It is the height of style in mid-Victorian
commercial design and expresses on the exterior its original
function. The rounded corner sets off its position on the south
west side of Walton and John Streets. The simple cornice with
projecting eaves lies over the second storey which is
inordinate in height, but this helps to balance it with its tall,
four storey neighbour to the west, the St. Lawrence Hotel.

It has three bays on Walton Street and five bays on John
Street on the second storey, the windows being large to light
the auditorium above. The smaller window on the rounded
corner was used for displaying signs for the Opera House. The
windows are elaborately outlined in ornamental brickwork
and archways springing from a band course carrying across
the pilasters, separating the recessed panels.

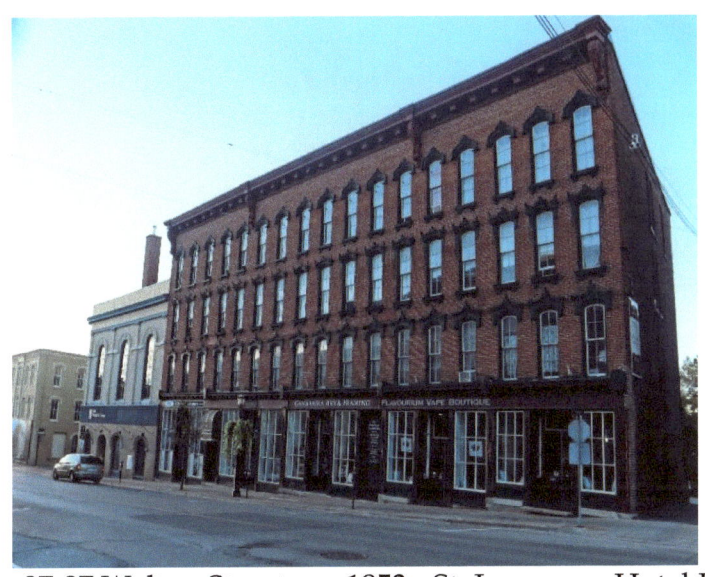

87-97 Walton Street – c. 1853 - St. Lawrence Hotel Block - It is a brick commercial building, four storeys high in five units and has seventeen bays to the main facade. It was designed for use as a hotel by American architect, Merwin Austin. Cast iron is used extensively on the front window labels and columns to the shop fronts. A heavy bracketed cornice fronts a low-sloped shed roof.

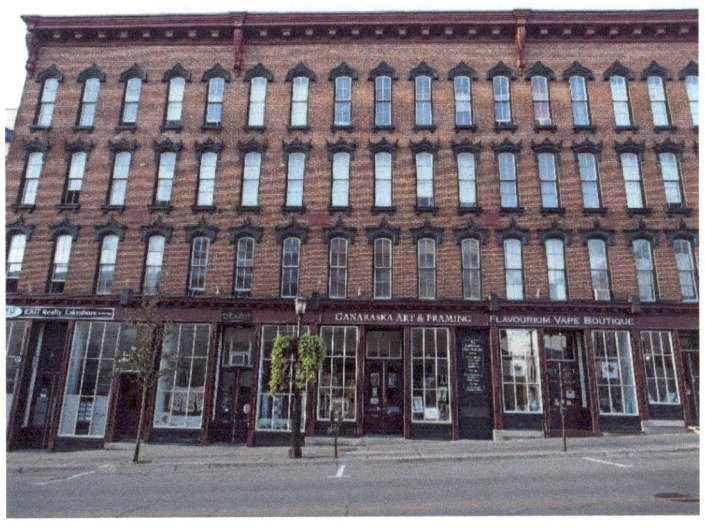

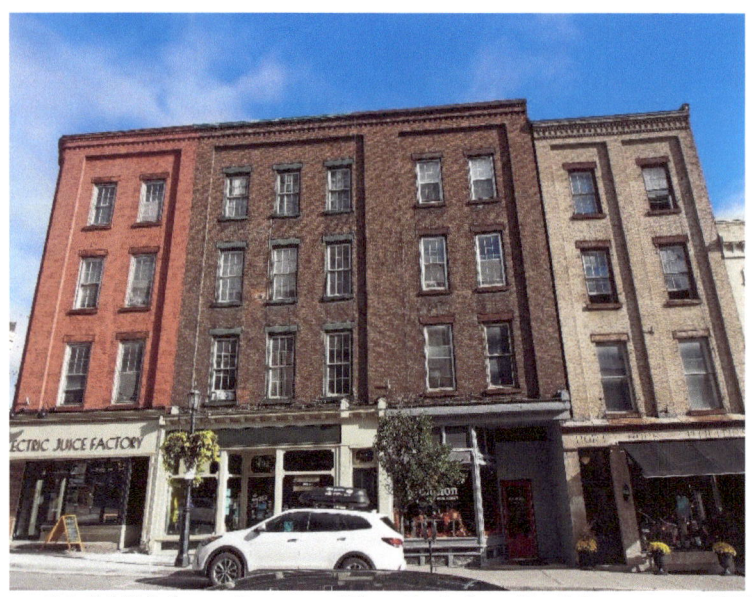

94-96 Walton Street – The Quinlan Building - c. 1855 - two-bay, four-storey building in light brick, pilastered front and ornamental brick cornice - The original arrangement of the structure was a main floor devoted to retail use and other floors, including the basement, were used for storage accessible through a hatch in the centre of the floor. Goods were hauled up and down by a windlass mounted in the top floor.

98-106 Walton Street - Knowlson Block – c 1854 - This magnificent block at the intersection of Cavan Street is a pilastered design of great simplicity and strength, with an ornamental brick cornice to the parapet disguising the shed roof and the traditional rounded corner echoing the building opposite. The centre unit is three bays wide, all with original sash windows, cast iron lintels and sills in the upper storeys facing Walton Street. The block has broad recessed panels and pilaster design. The roof top cornice is formed by a row of stretchers, a row of dogtoothing, several courses of stretchers and then a course of dentilling.

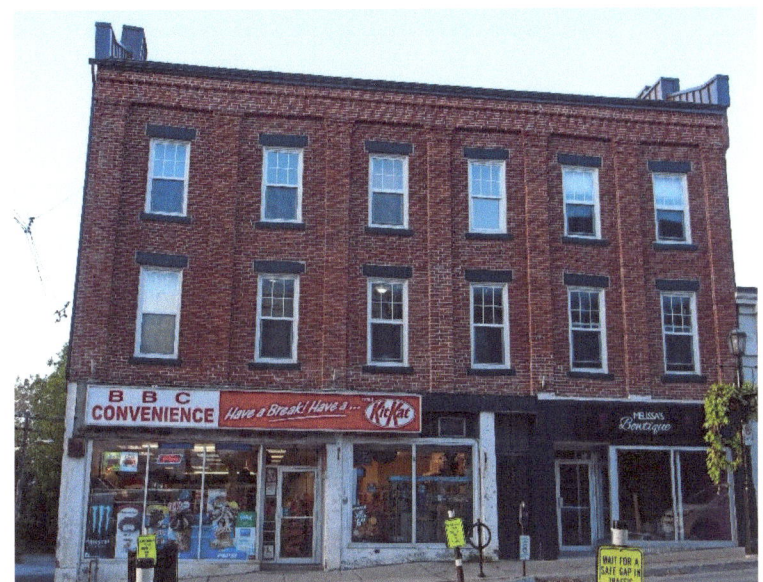

99-105 Walton Street

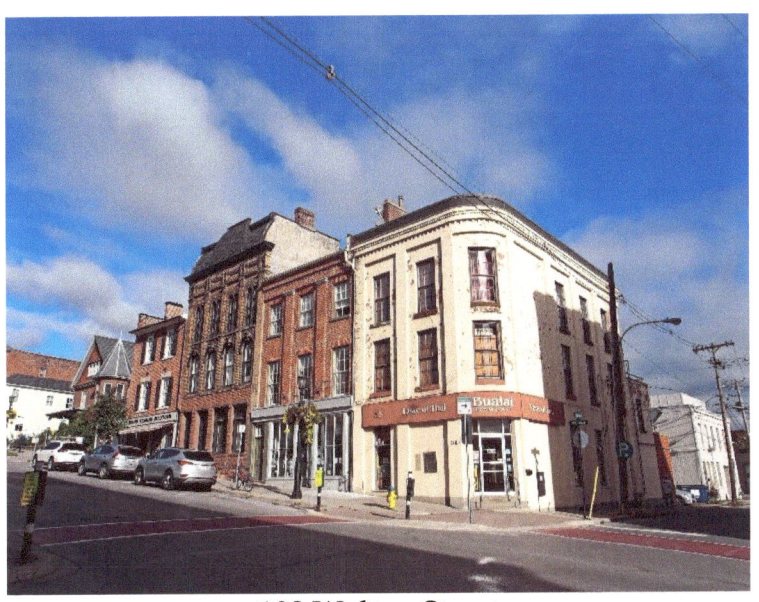

108 Walton Street

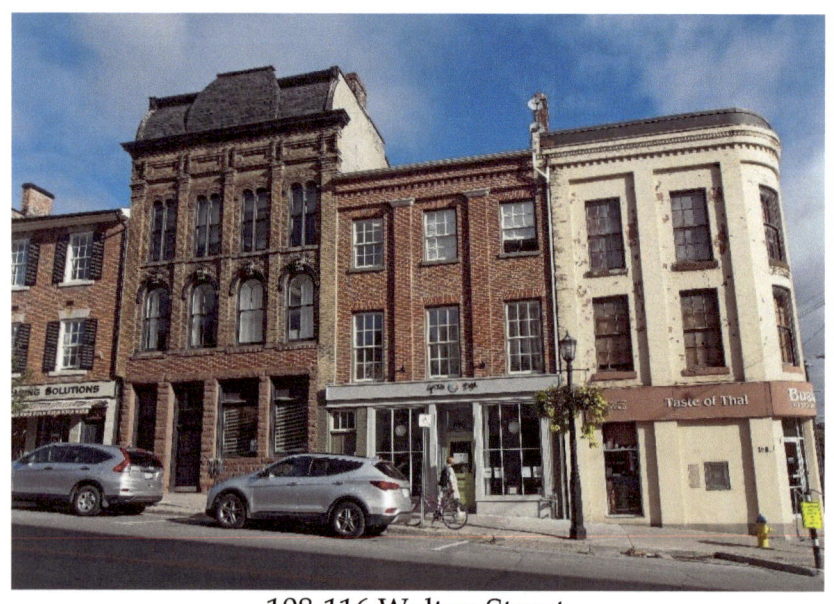
108-116 Walton Street

114-116 Walton Street - Russell Block – c. 1875 - This block is a three-storey Second Empire brick building, four bays wide with a false mansard roof. The second storey bays have semi-circular structural openings with decorative cast iron lintels. The third storey bays are twin semi-circular bays separated by narrow columns and featuring decorative brick lintels. The facade of the block is pilastered from the second storey to about one and a half feet above the third storey bays. There are two large pilasters on either end topped with decorative brick capitals. The facade has a machicolated brick cornice with recessed panels below the wooden cornice of the roof. Henry C. Russell (1834-1911) was a cabinetmaker and furniture dealer.

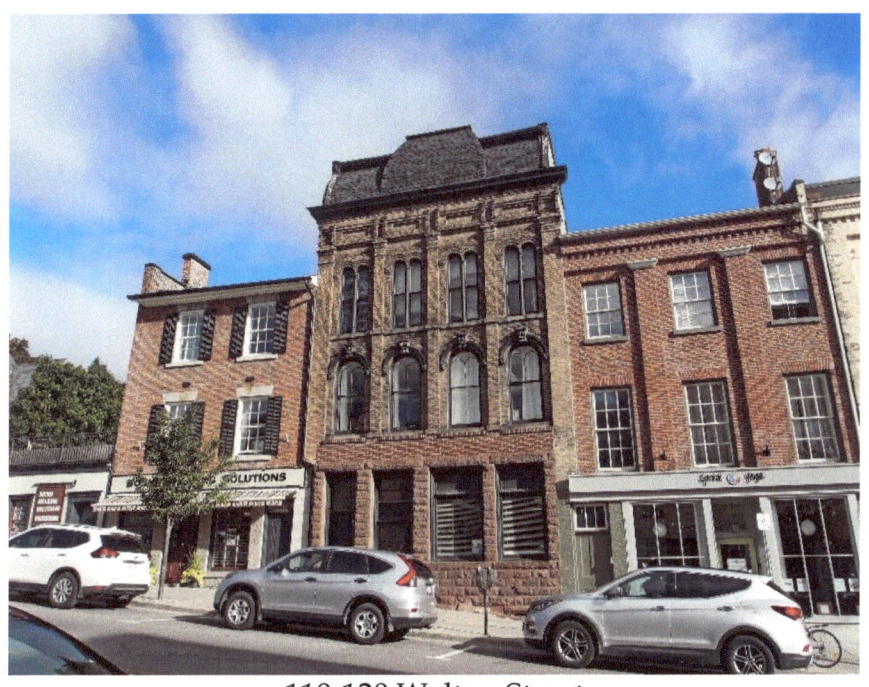
110-120 Walton Street
118-120 Walton Street – c. 1841 – The Guide Office -
This is the oldest surviving structure in the commercial section
of Walton Street. This three-storey brick building has a gable
roof, parallel to the street, with parapet walls.

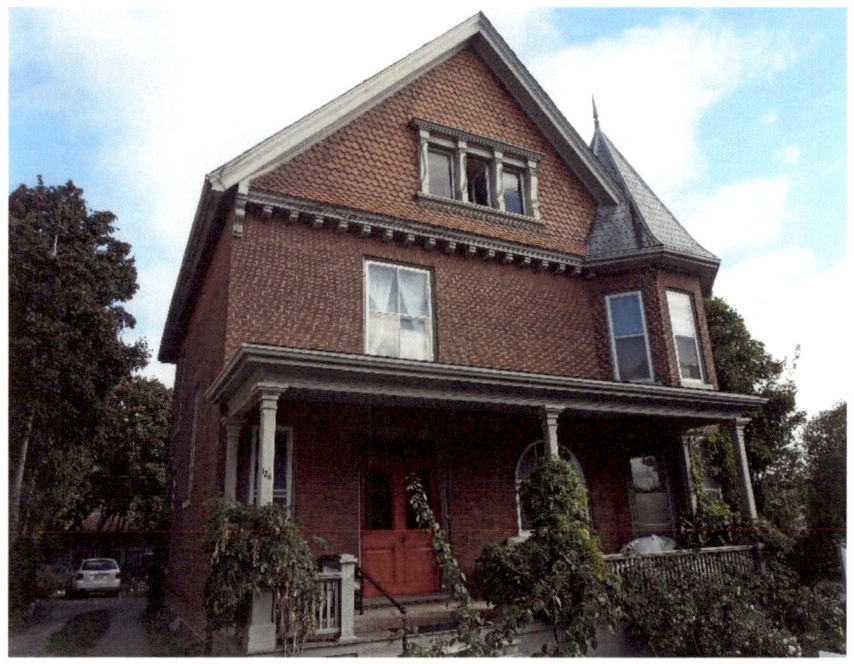

126 Walton Street - Wilson-Benson House – c. 1885 -
This two and a half storey brick house is built in the Queen
Anne Revival style with an offset tower, a broad verandah,
and a steeply pitched roof. The gable on the Walton Street
facade is sheathed in decorative shingle. The tower is five-
sided with a conical roof topped by a finial and contains a
long window on each storey of each wall surface. The large
main floor window is Edwardian in treatment with coloured
glass in the semi-circular transom section.

For fifty years, the Wilsons were publishers of the Port
Hope Guide.

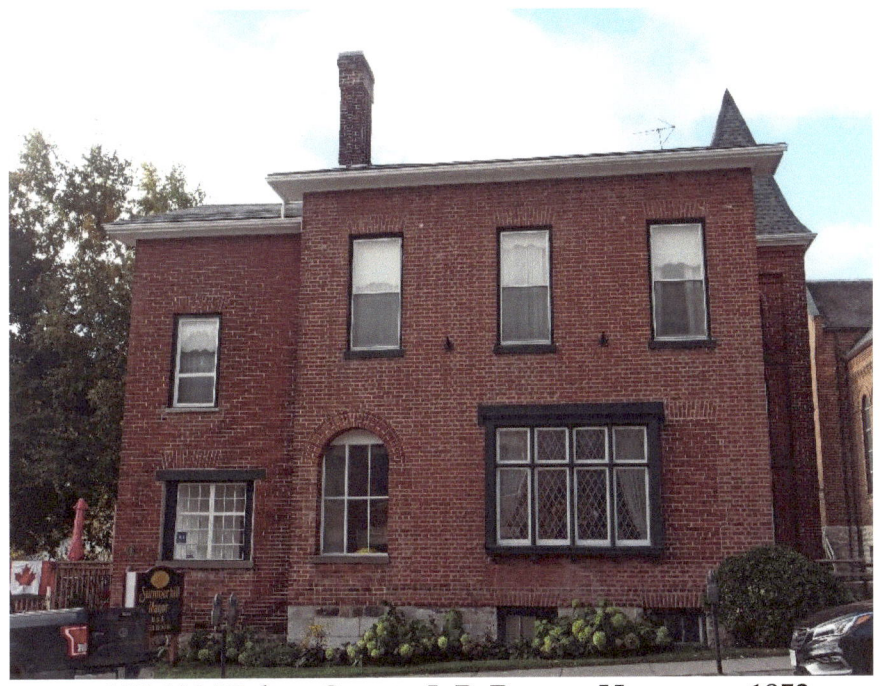

127-129 Walton Street - L.B. Powers House – c. 1853 (modified 1878) - From 1878 to 1930 this building was the residence of the prominent physician. Dr. L. B. Powers. It is a two and a half storey brick home. The raised roof is of moderate pitch, and a hipped-roofed, three storey brick tower was added on the west wall.

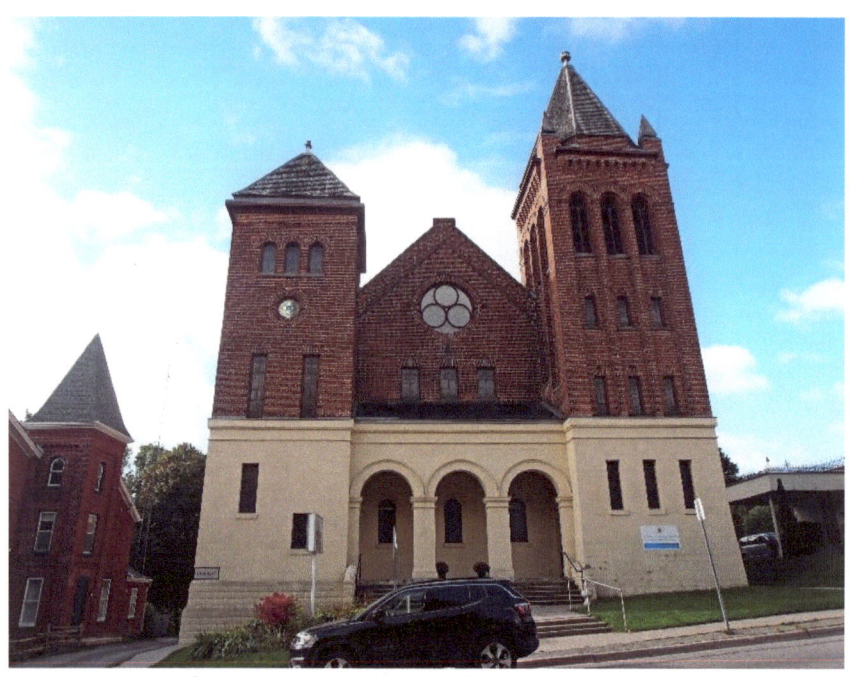

131 Walton Street – St. Paul's Presbyterian Church – c. 1906 – This is brick over a cast stone base and, essentially, of the Romanesque Revival style. Massive towers frame the front with an arcaded porch between sheltering the tower entrances and above, the gabled front to the sanctuary and its rear gallery. Windows to towers display simple stained glass in Art Nouveau designs, the taller west tower with louvred openings to the bell stage and with a short spire above. The shorter east tower has a hipped roof. The chimney is a massive shaft very much contributing to the architectural silhouette. A fine rose window, also exhibiting Art Nouveau designs, dominates the front gable but lights only the loft space above the sanctuary.

Brickwork has ornamentation in hood moulds over windows, a corbelled frieze and pilasters.

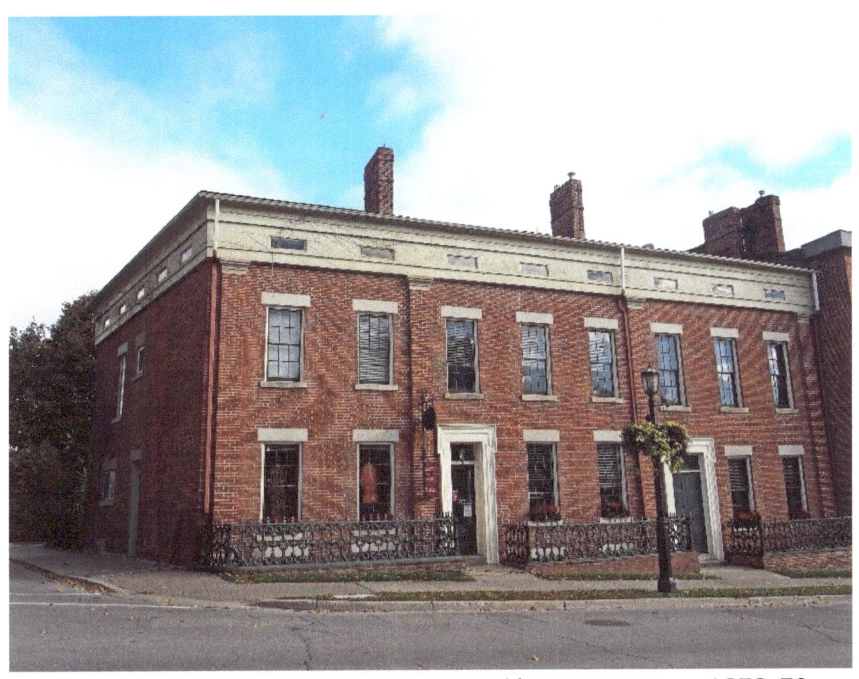

134-136 Walton Street - Metcalfe Terrace – c. 1852-53 - This two-storey terrace embraces most of the features typical of the Greek Revival style: brick pilasters, heavy entablature punctuated by stomachers in the frieze. It is constructed of brick laid in Flemish bond and is divided by brick pilasters into three sections of irregular size. The middle section has three bays on both storeys of the main façade.

The side of the building fronting on Brown Street shows evidence of earlier window openings that have been bricked over.

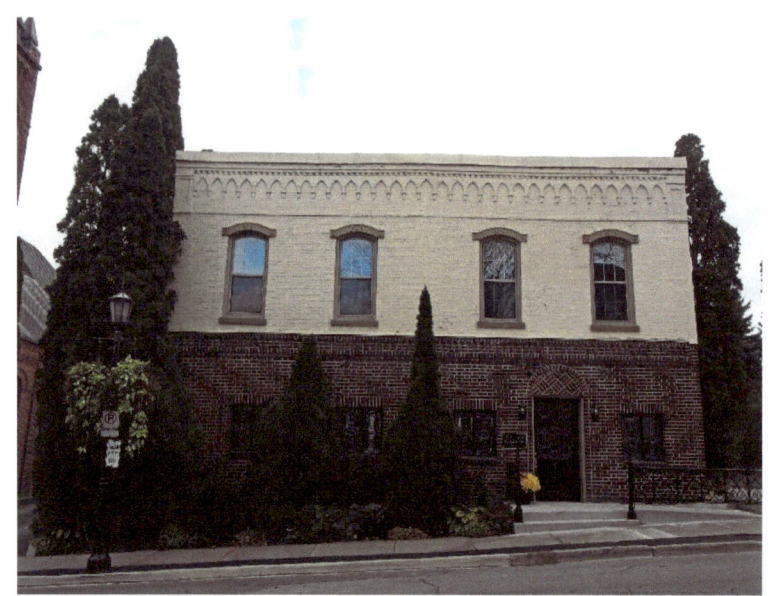

135 Walton Street – W.C. Ross Funeral Chapel – decorative cornice

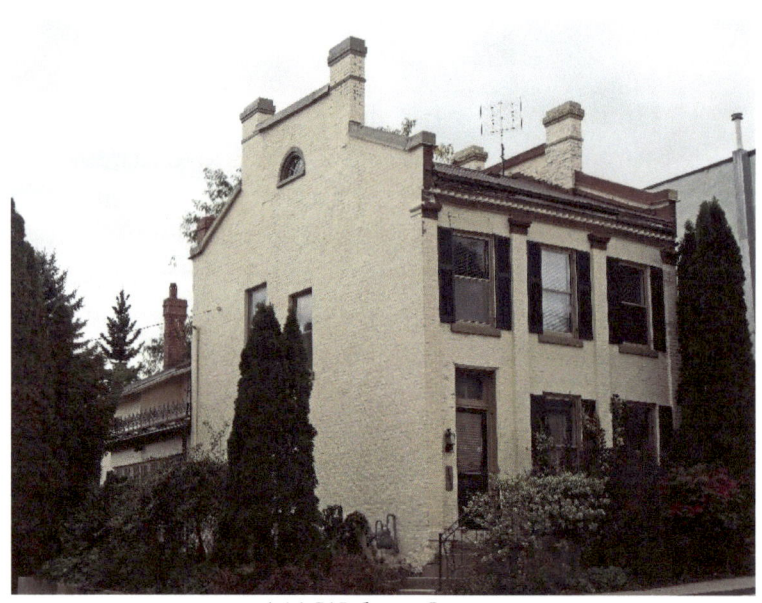

141 Walton Street

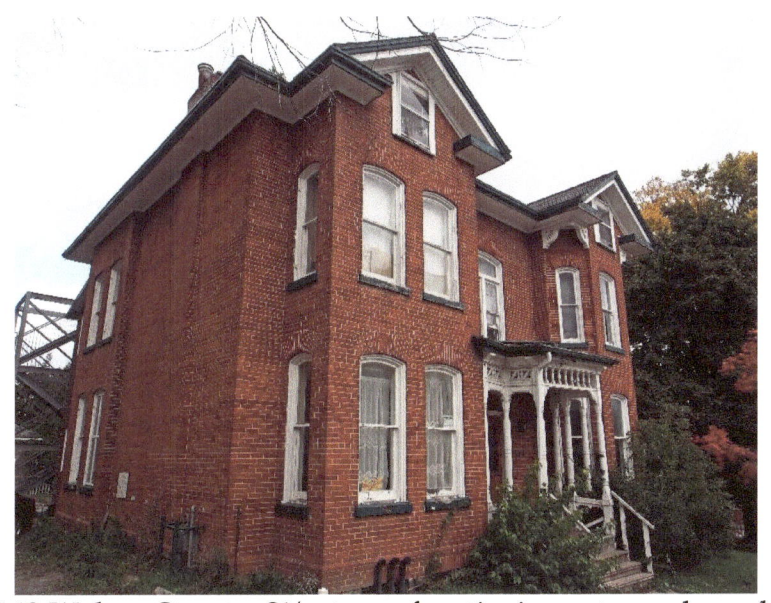

142 Walton Street – 2½-storey frontispieces, turned porch supports

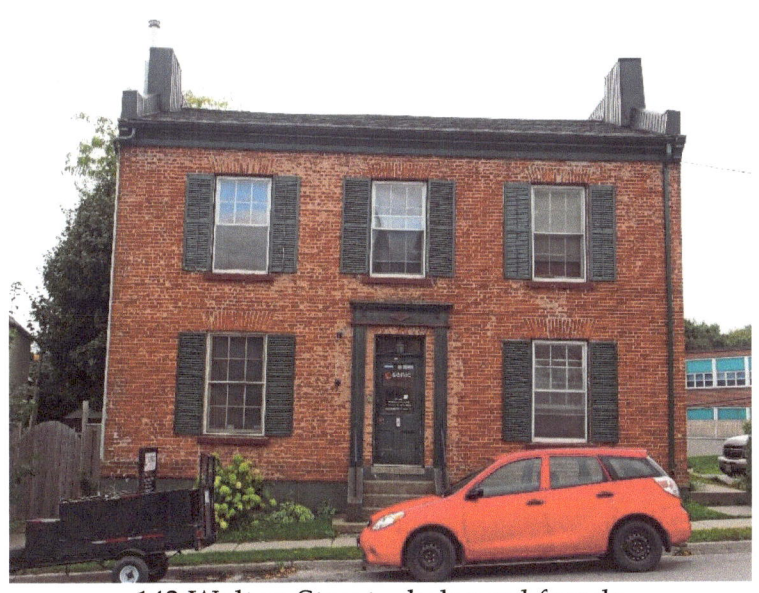

143 Walton Street – balanced façade

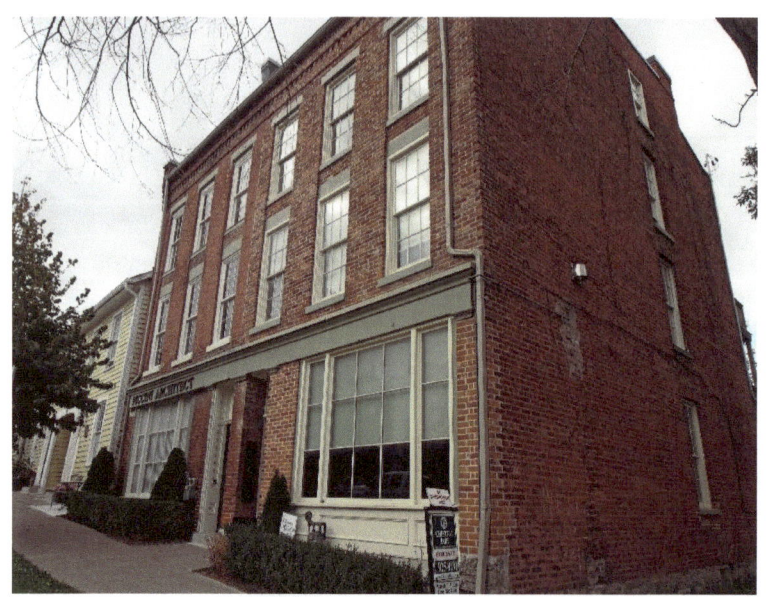

148 Walton Street

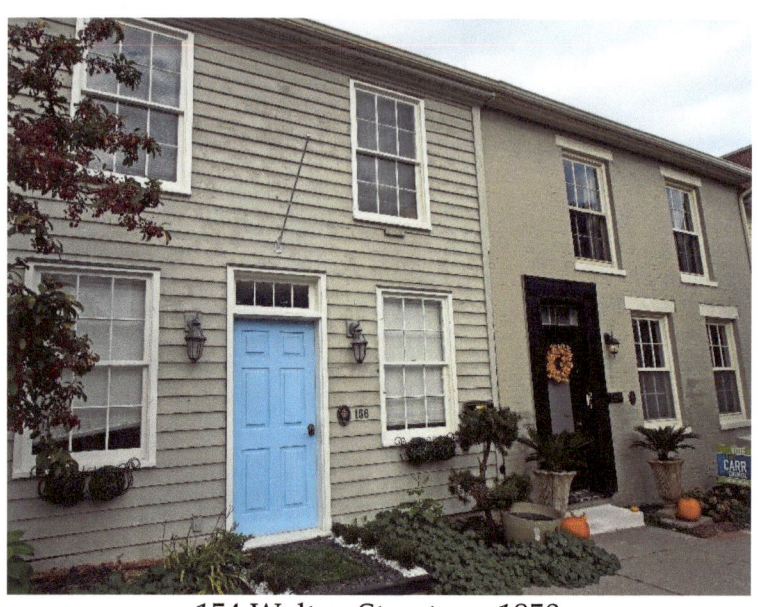

154 Walton Street – c. 1850
156 Walton Street – c. 1852

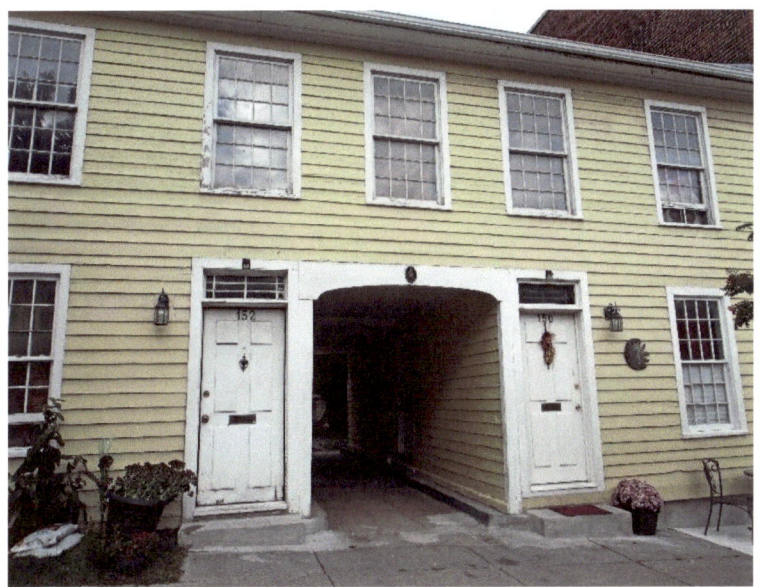

150-152 Walton Street - Misson Duplex = c. 1843 - This early Neo-Classical vernacular building with a carriageway in the middle is rectangular in plan. There are four bays on the first floor and five on the second, with flat wooden surrounds. The roof is moderately pitched with a plain-boxed cornice and plain frieze. The building is now divided into two dwellings with side entrances. The building is of frame construction. The gently curved arch over the carriageway is connected to the transoms over the two rather narrow doors.

Richard Misson (1816-1891) was born in Lincolnshire, England in 1816 and emigrated to Canada in 1836. He established himself as a painter and later partnered with Richard Fogarty as Misson & Fogarty, painters and paperhangers. In 1845, he built the Customs House (12 Mill Street South). In 1853, he established a sash factory. By 1859, his eleven-year partnership with Fogarty had dissolved. By 1880, Richard Misson is listed in local directories as a gentleman residing on Mill Street perhaps at 12 Mill Street South.

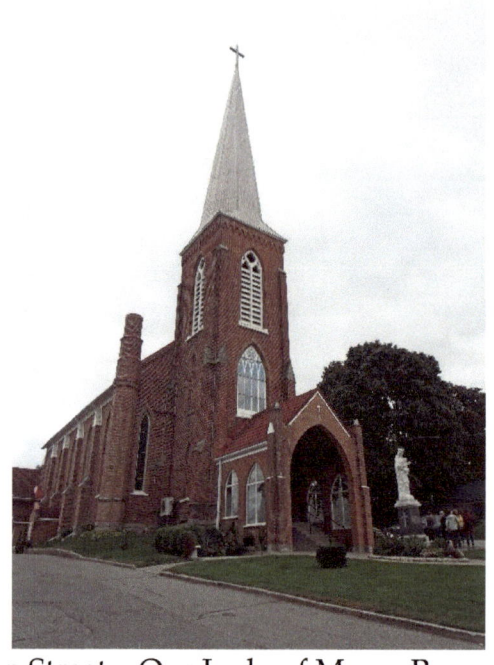

155 Walton Street – Our Lady of Mercy Roman Catholic Church

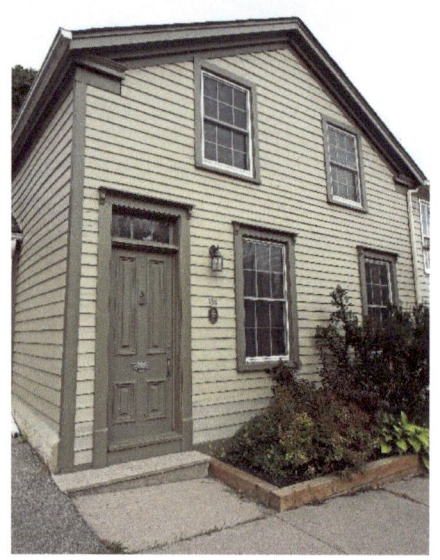

158 Walton Street – c. 1843-45

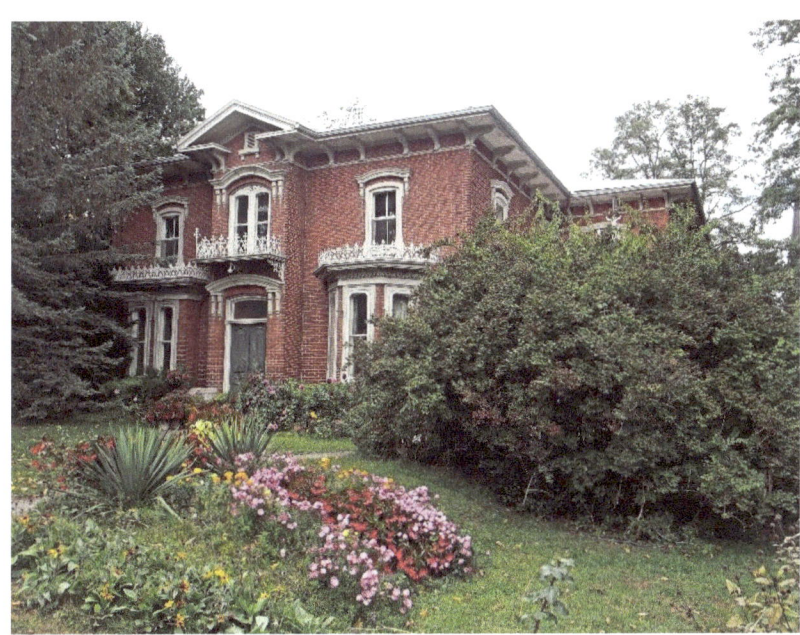

Walton Street – Italianate style – iron cresting above bay windows and entrance, cornice brackets

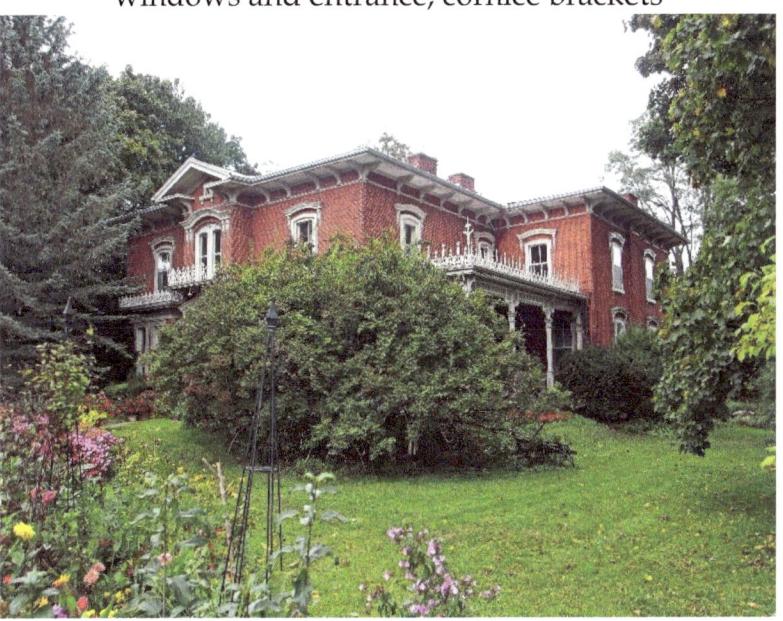

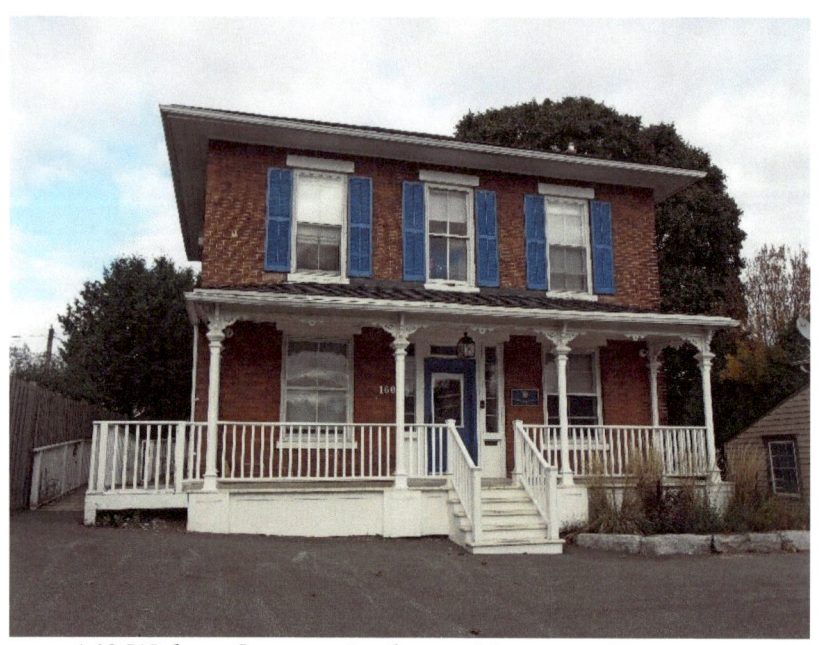

160 Walton Street - Andrews Newman House – c. 1852 - This two-storey, rectangular, brick-veneered house with medium-pitched roof with a flat centre deck has three bays to both storeys on the main facade. The windows have plain lintels and lugsills and are shuttered on the second storey. A verandah runs across the front of the house, supported by turned wooden supports and decorative bargeboard. The door has a flat transom and sidelights.

The larger front windows on the ground floor with recessed doorcase with sidelights and transom indicate this building may have started out as an Ontario Cottage. The first storey windows are wider than the second storey, and the lugsills narrower than those of the second storey.

Joseph Newman (1813-1859) was originally from Ireland, having arrived in Port Hope about 1838 or perhaps earlier. He was a baker, grocer and dealer in country produce with a shop on Walton Street.

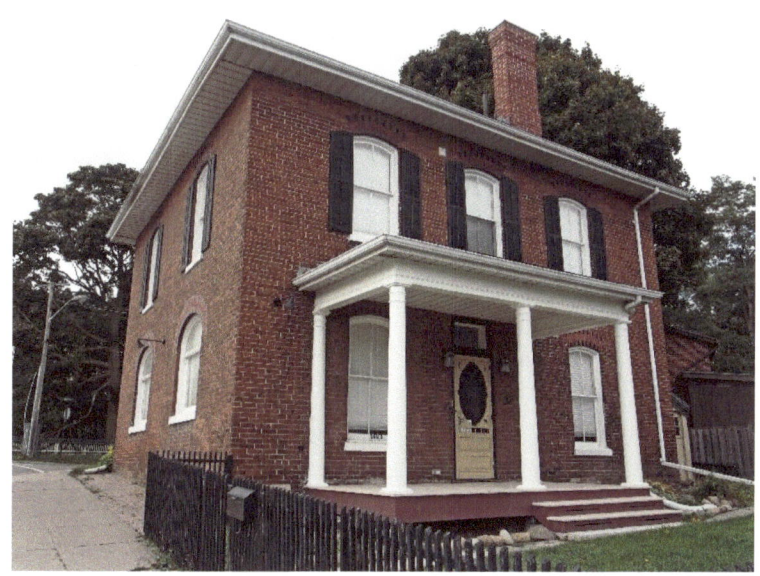

162 Walton Street – c. 1888 - George Hooker House - Built originally as a two-storey shop and dwelling, this square house is constructed of brick laid in stretcher bond and has a medium-pitched hipped roof with a flat deck and plain-boxed cornice. On the east wall, where the main door is located, there are three bays on both storeys. The windows have segmental heads with radiating brick arches, painted lugsills, and well-fitting shutters. A porch with five supporting columns is located off-centre on the east wall.

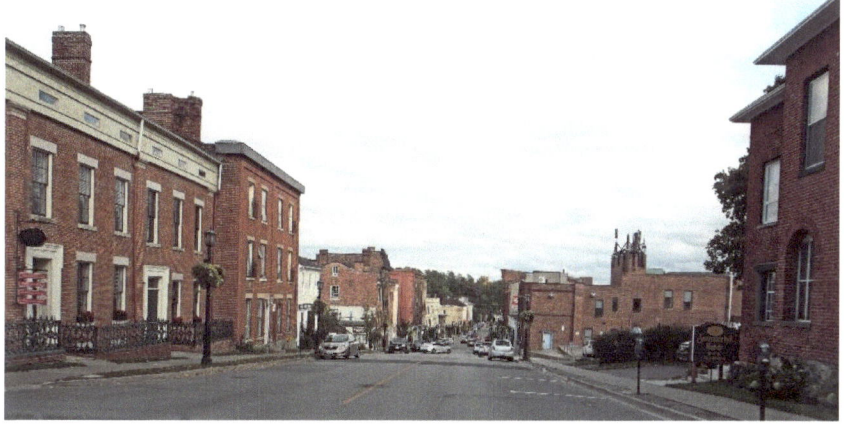

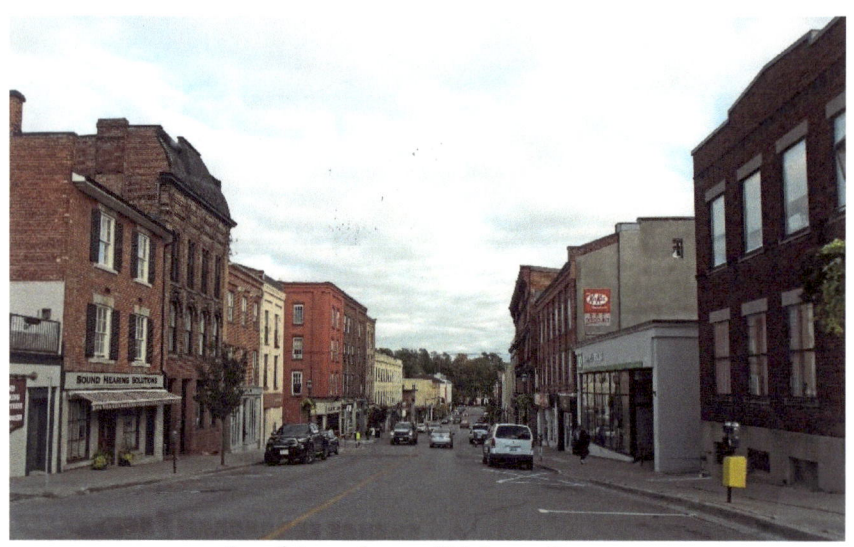

Looking down Walton Street

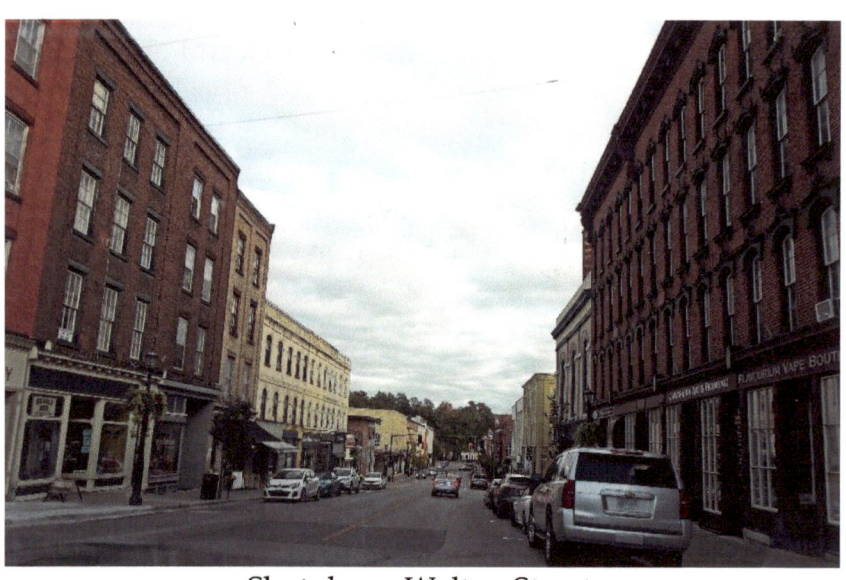

Shot down Walton Street

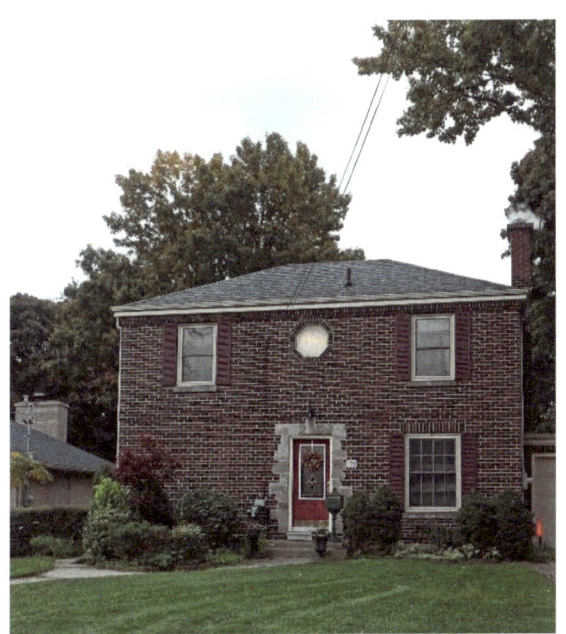

179 Walton Street

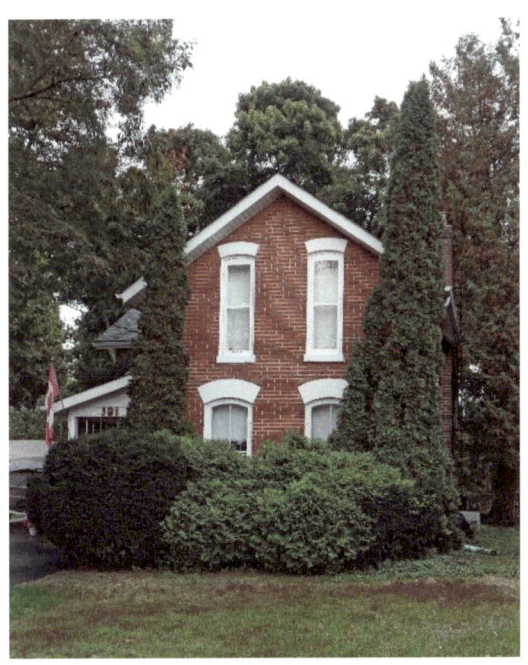

181 Walton Street

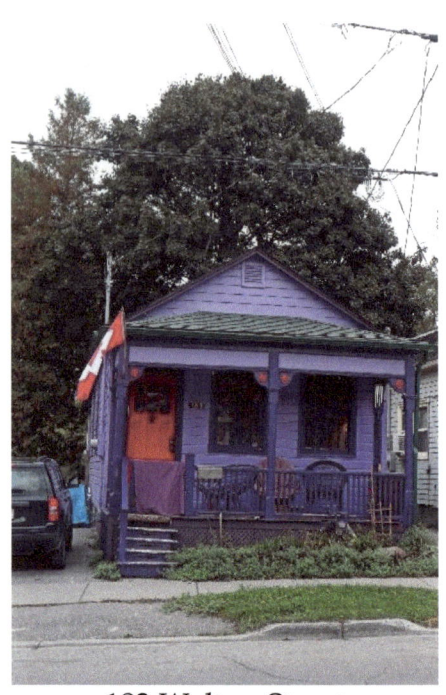

183 Walton Street

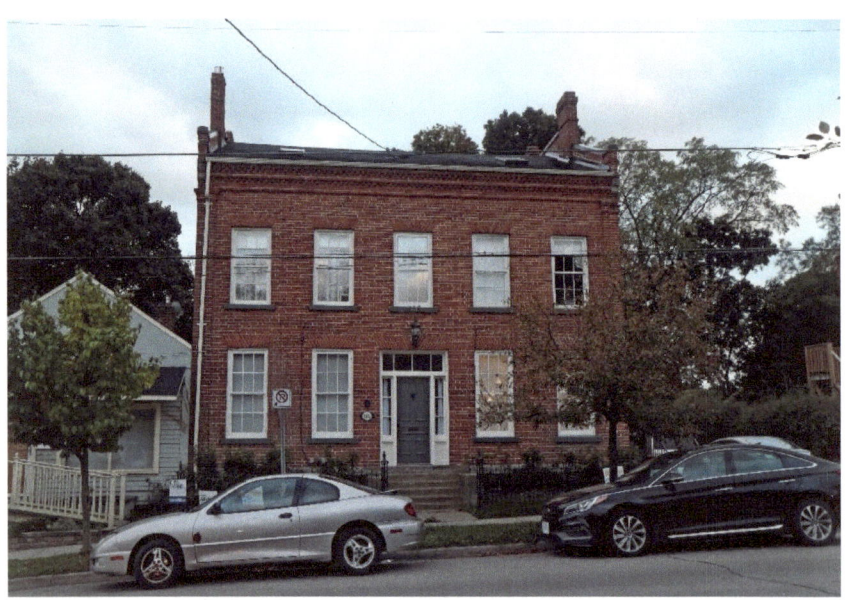

187 Walton Street – Victorian Town House

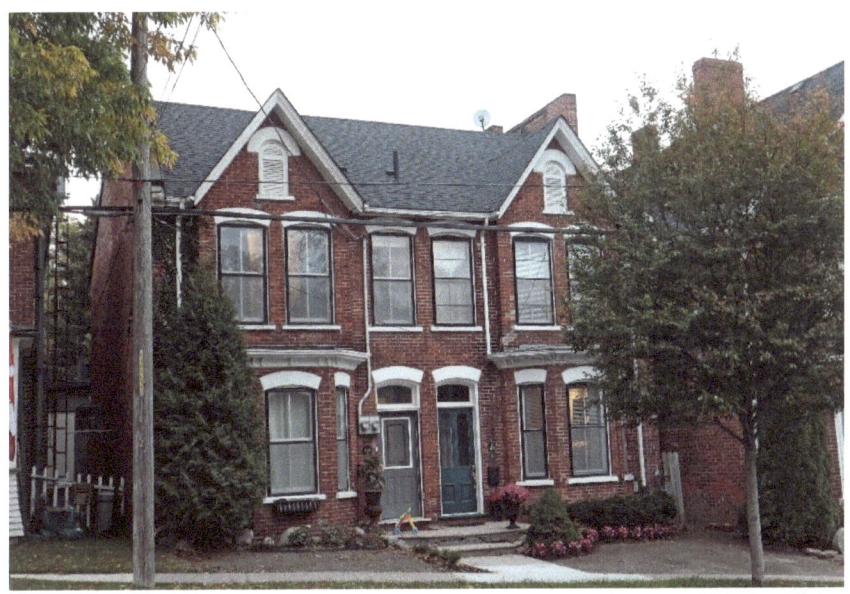

186-184 Walton Street - Williams Duplex- c. 1875 - This is a duplex, standing two-storeys high with a gable roof. The composition is enhanced by a gabled "frontispiece", which projects slightly from the facade. This in turn is graced by a bay window (at ground level), complete with cornice and brackets. At second-floor level, the "frontispiece" bears two windows. All the bays are segmentally arched, except the louvred attic vent, which is round arched.

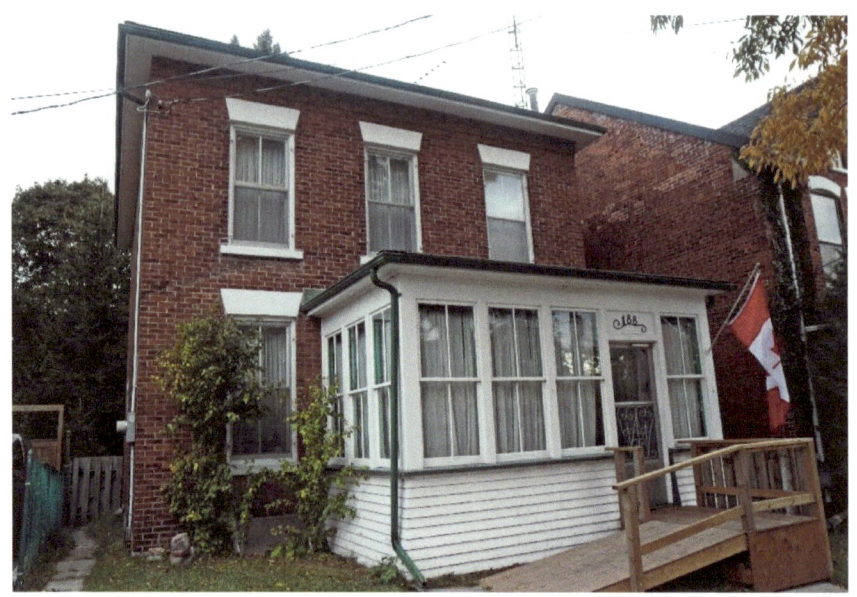

188 Walton Street

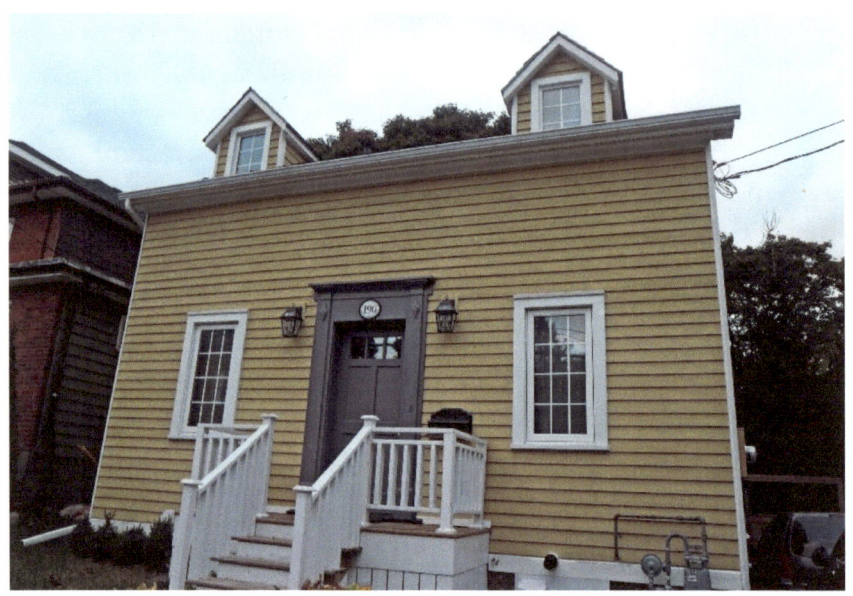

190 Walton Street – dormers on roof

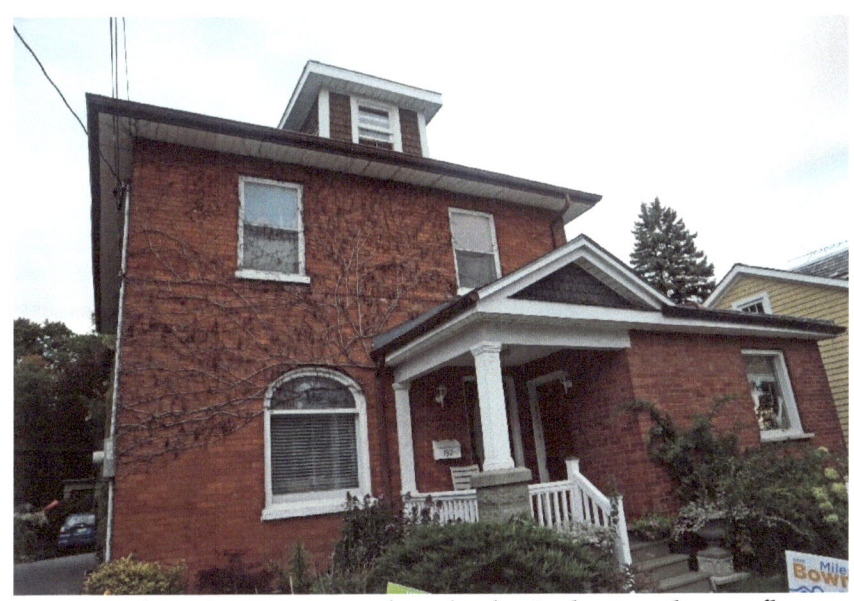

192 Walton Street – round-arched window on lower floor

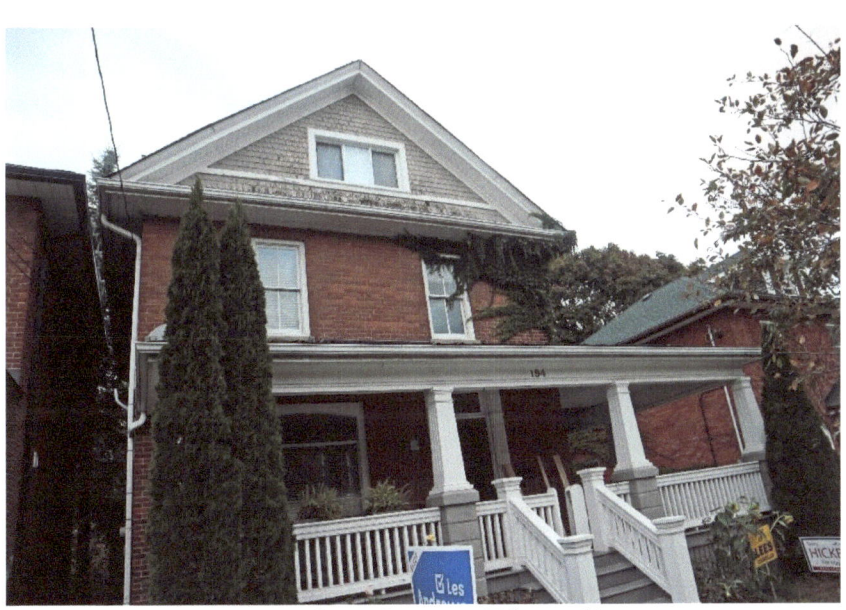

194 Walton Street - Edwardian

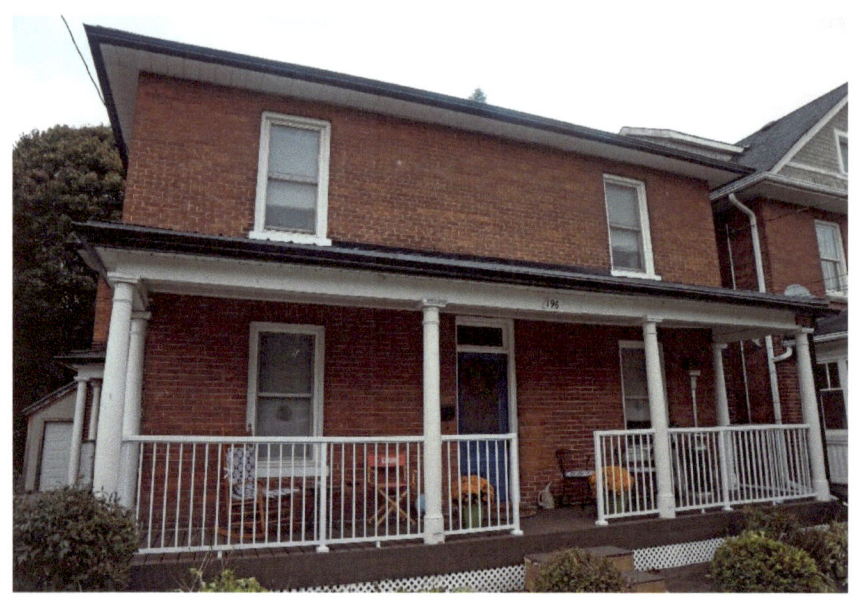

196 Walton Street

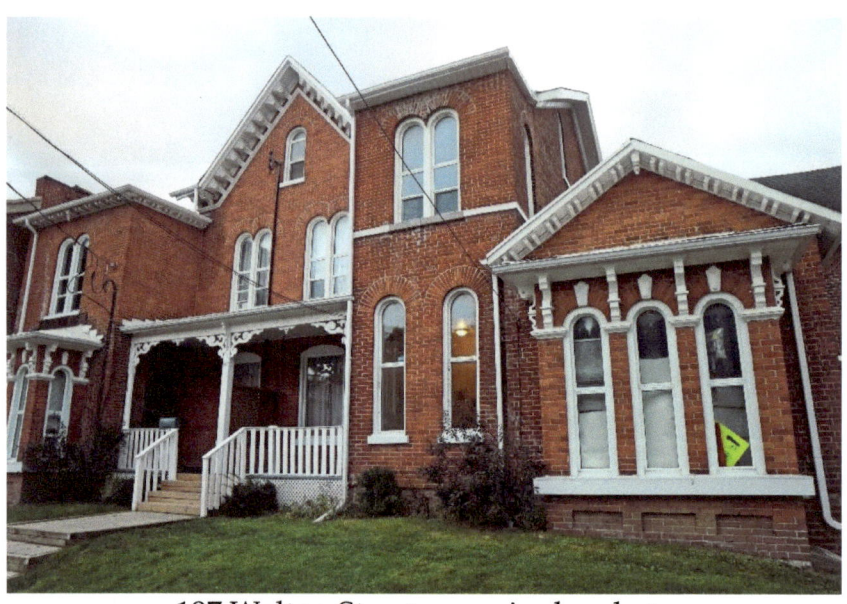

197 Walton Street – cornice brackets

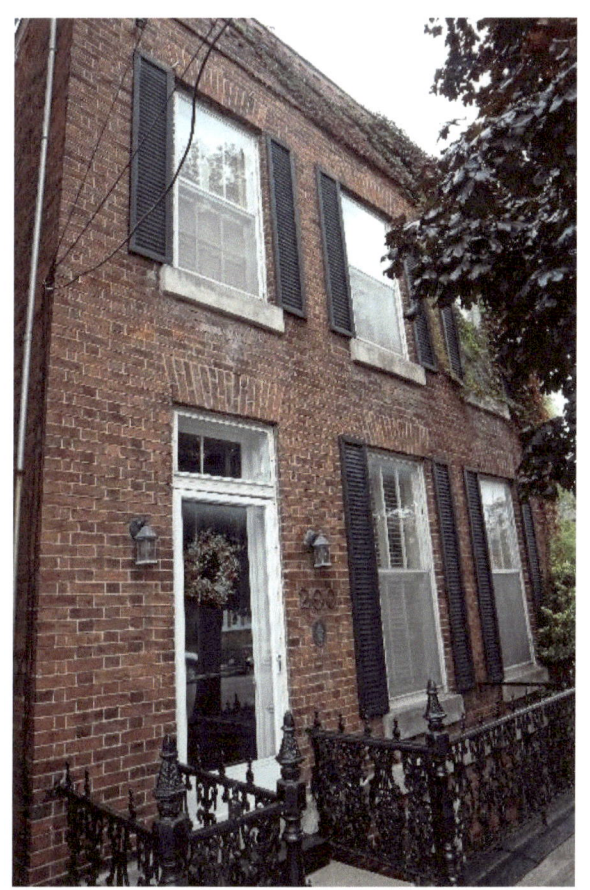

200 Walton Street – c. 1850 - James Sculthorpe
Townhouse - flat shed roof - The house stands two storeys
high at front; the lot slopes to the rear, allowing the basement
to open at ground level at the back. The medium is brick, with
a Flemish bond facade. There is a patterned brick cornice. The
facade has three bays; the sides are blind.

The cast-iron fence, with its lyre shaped pattern,
cordons off the tiny front yard. It is a rare example of the
founder's art.

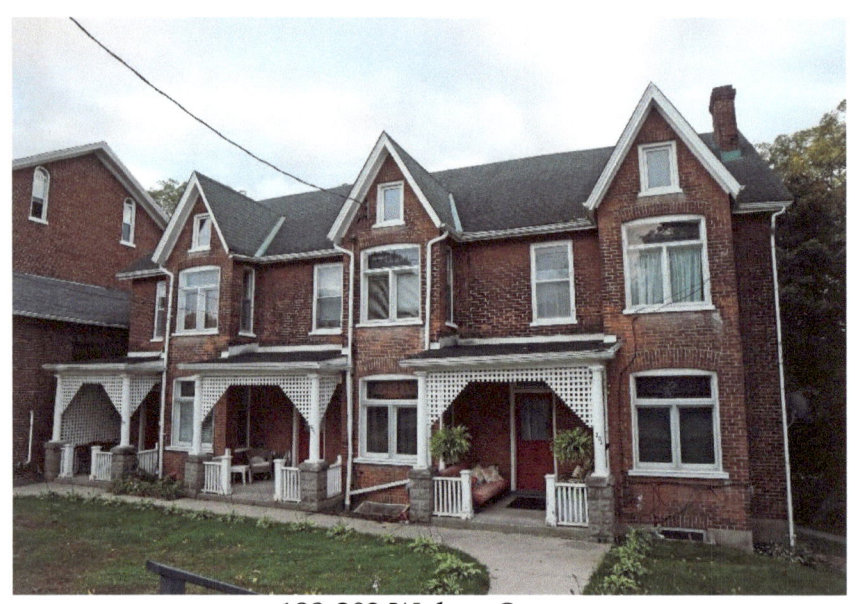

199-203 Walton Street

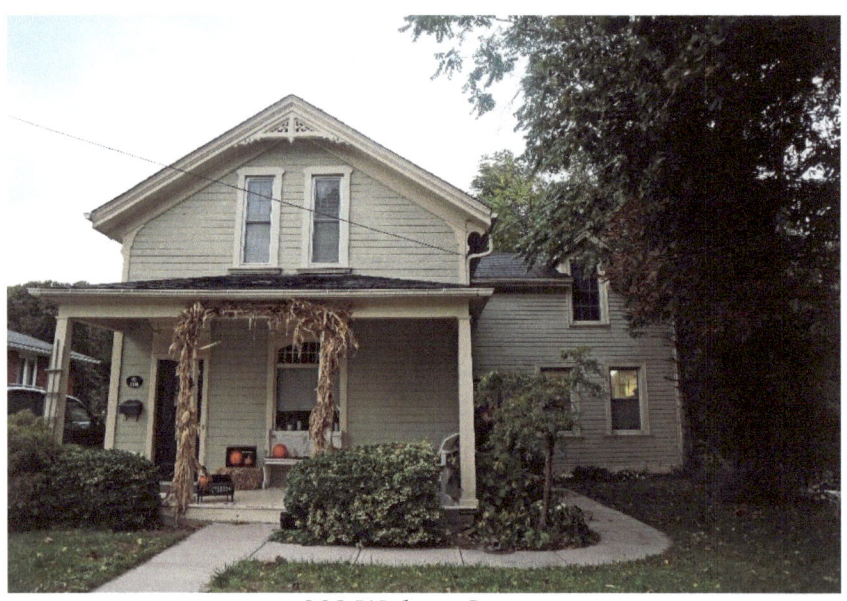

208 Walton Street

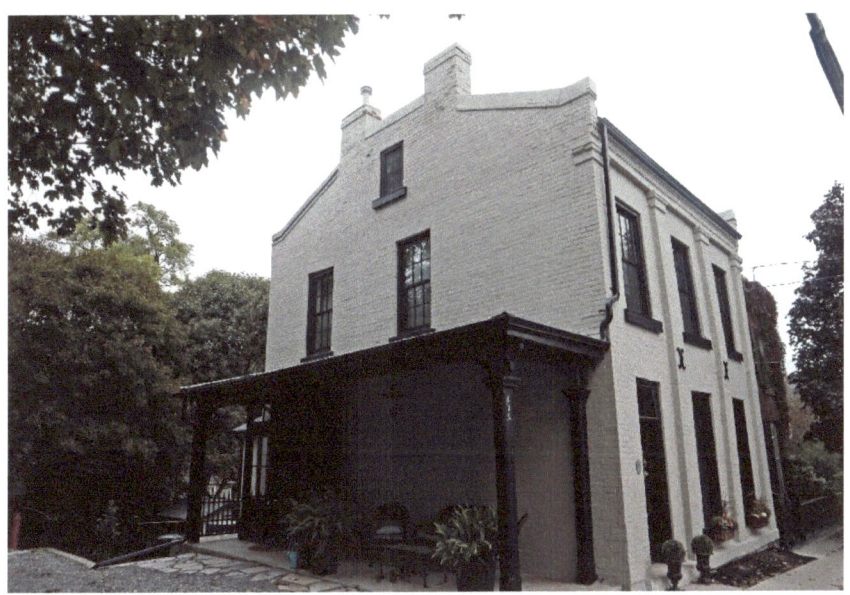

202 Walton Street – c. 1850 - McDougall Smart House - It is a vernacular house with an interesting main facade. The roof has a parapet gable roof trim, and it has no overhang where it slopes down on the north and south sides. Four single chimneys, two on either side of the gable peak, emerge from the parapet trim. The main facade has six openings: there are three equally spaced windows on the second floor, and directly below are two more windows and the new front door with its single sash transom above. There are four pilasters; just below the roof line, some brick dentations decorate the wall's surface.

Around the back door there is a small inner closed porch composed of panels of wood and glass divided by chamfered strappings. A large porch extends over this and down to the road. It has an elevated concrete floor on which stands four columns: these columns are square-based and have bevelled edges. They are crowned with simple capitals, and from these, decorative supports and small brackets extend up to the roof.

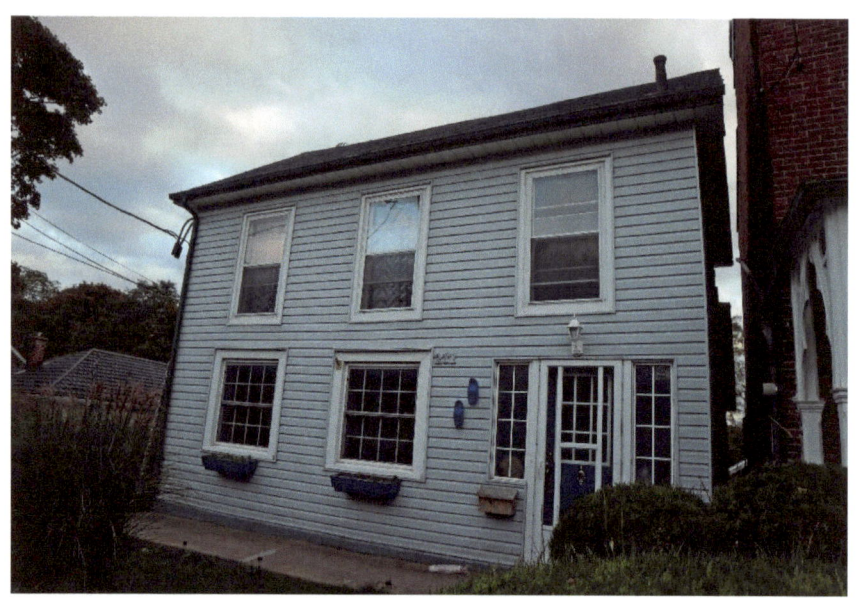

211 Walton Street

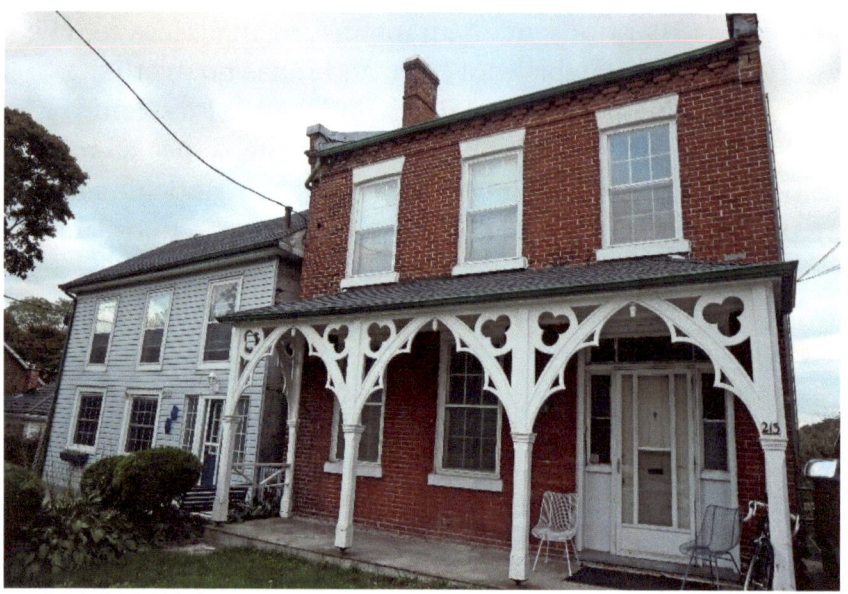

211-213 Walton Street – decorative porch supports with trefoils

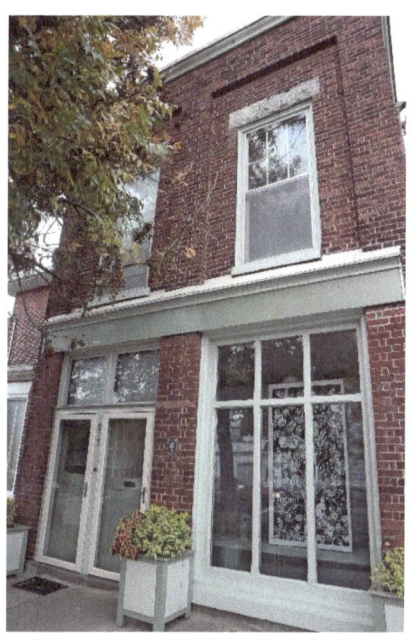

217 Walton Street – c. 1850 - Englishtown Firehall - This is a large two-storey brick structure with a sloping shed-style roof. The lot slopes to the rear, leaving the casement exposed at the back of the property. The block adopts a commercial form with its brick-pilastered façade. In lieu of shop fronts, the ground floor has two wide bays, which presumably owe their form to the building's original function as a fire hall. The upper storey has two tall evenly spaced windows with six-over-six sash.

Organized by members of the community, the fire company was comprised of volunteers. During this period, only manual pumps were available and these required large crews to keep the handles that operated the pumps manned. There were no horses connected with this fire hall. The pumpers had handles at each end and were pulled and pushed by firemen. The Firehall is located on the western most section of Walton Street in the area referred to as Englishtown near where the street name changes from Walton to Ridout.

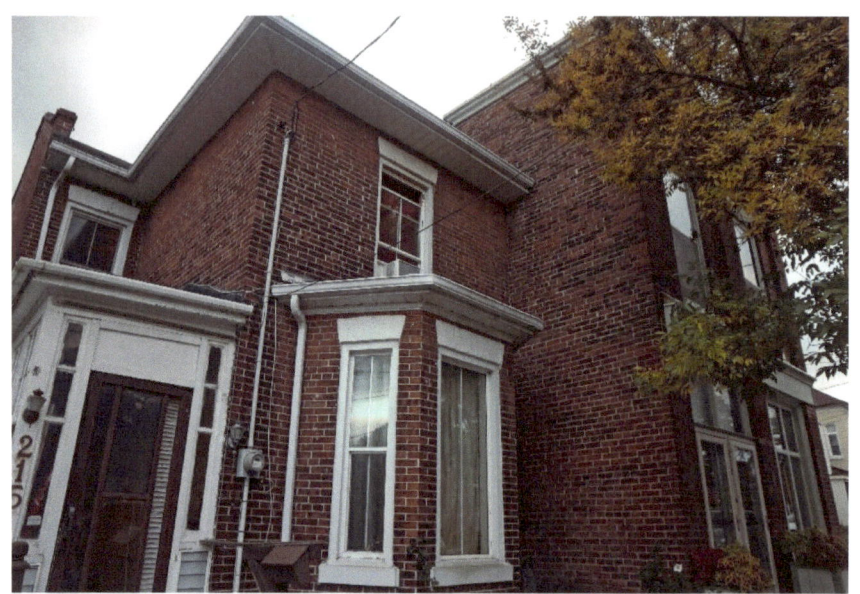
215 Walton Street – bay window

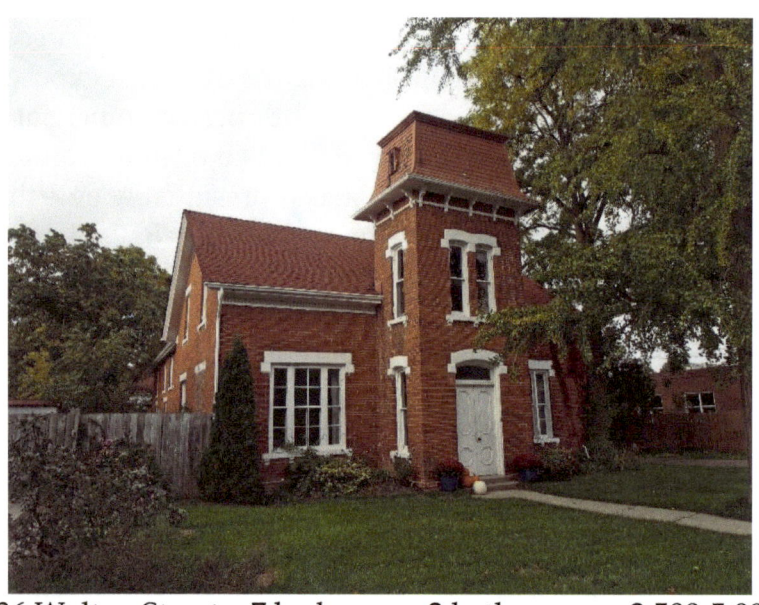
236 Walton Street – 7 bedrooms, 2 bathrooms – 3,500-5,000 square feet – 2½-storey tower with mansard roof, cornice brackets

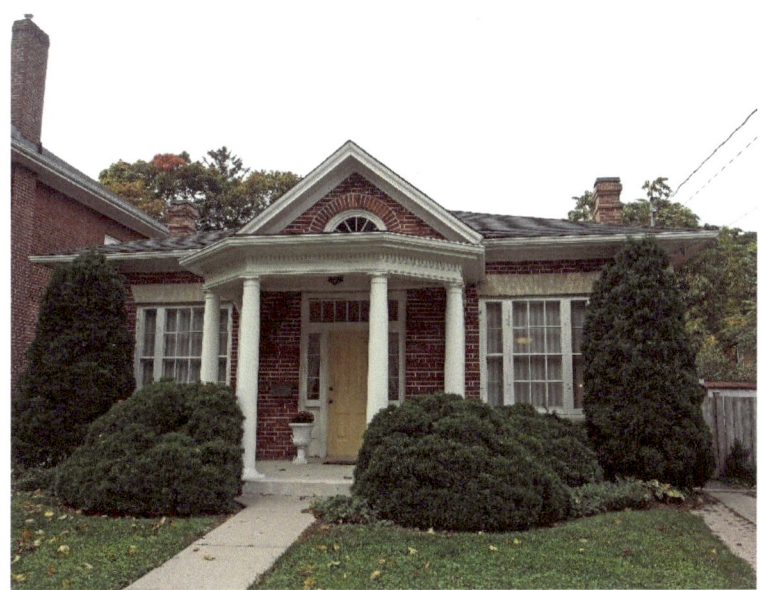

238 Walton Street - semi-circular radiating fan window in the gable above the porch, sidelights, transom

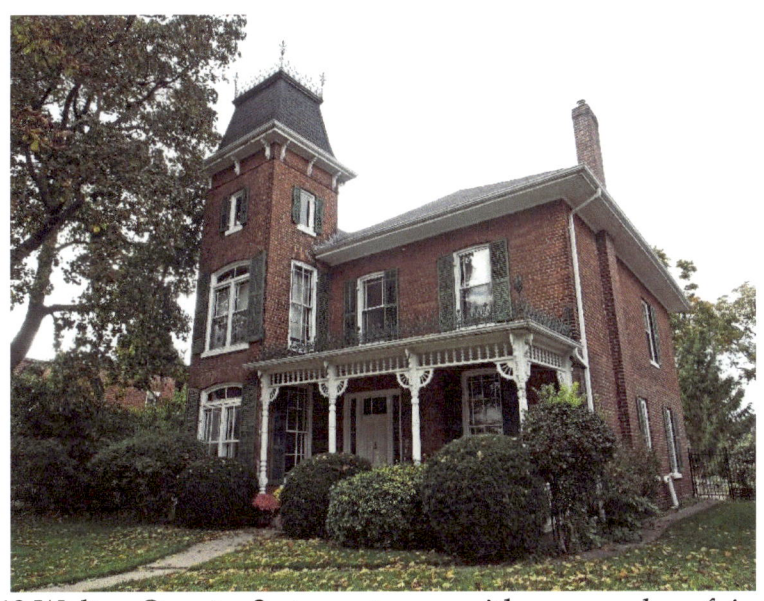

240 Walton Street – 3-storey tower with mansard roof, iron cresting, cornice brackets spindles and decorative porch supports

Other Books by Barbara Raue

Coins of Gold
Arrows, Indians and Love
The Life and Times of Barbara
The Cromwell Family Book
Laura Secord Discovered
Daddy Where Are You?

Montana Series
Book 1: Montana Dream
Book 2: Life on the Montana Frontier
Book 3: Montana to Boston and Back
Book 4: Montana Sons Go to War
Book 5: Montana Sons Return from War

www.ingramcontent.com/pod-product-compliance
Lightning Source LLC
Chambersburg PA
CBHW041106180526
45172CB00001B/125